DRUG EDUCATION

A Bibliography
of Available Inexpensive Materials

compiled by

DOROTHY P. WELLS

The Scarecrow Press, Inc.
Metuchen, N.J.   1972

Library of Congress Cataloging in Publication Data

Wells, Dorothy Pearl, 1910-
    Drug education.

    1. Drug abuse--Bibliography. 2. Drugs--Biblio-
graphy. I. Title.
Z7164.N17W45   016.3622'93   72-317
ISBN 0-8108-0507-3

CONTENTS

iii

PREFACE

The following bibliography on drug education materialized as the result of an effort to supply the demand of college students for pamphlet items in the vertical file. One source led to another and resulted in a wide variety of publishers, a wide range of length of individual items--from broadsides to books over 150 pages--and costs varying from free to $2.50.

Although there is considerable repetition of information to be found in the content of the entries, the presentations and insights vary, aiding one's broadened conception of the drug abuse dilemma. Views emanate from the legal, medical, law enforcement, ministerial, educational, governmental, pharmaceutical, and social professions. And there seems to be a message for all ages and points of view. However, general information suitable for high school students and adults predominates, i.e., cause and prevention of the problem, how to recognize hard drug users, basic facts about drugs themselves, legal controls, and treatment. Material for the elementary school child appears to be limited.

Mention has been made of some teachers' handbooks and curriculum guides which are available, although with one exception no material of this type has specifically been cited unless it also serves as a basic resource. Single copies of that particular curricular item cited (item No. 145) are available free from the National Clearinghouse for Drug Abuse Education.

Pamphlets listed in a bibliography, "Drug Education," dated March 17, 1971, and received from the U.S. Government Printing Office, have been included, along with a few other government documents, not all of which have been annotated since there were a few unavailable to the compiler. And possibly some of the items listed will not be available at the time this book goes to press should the stock have become exhausted.

The National Institute of Mental Health, Clinical Research Center, Leestown Pike, Lexington, Kentucky, 40507, advised the compiler by letter that their Center may be listed as a source of free material in the drug abuse field. This material changes periodically because of revisions and shortages of copies and also when new publications become available. A free publication on "Argot in Use by the Drug Abuser" and another on evaluating audio-visual materials about drug abuse will be available very soon. Representative free pamphlets were also received from the U.S. Department of Health, Education and Welfare and from the Bureau of Narcotics and Dangerous Drugs.

No effort was made to ferret out magazine article reprints on the subject of drug abuse. Those included came in unsolicited, or were cited in other bibliographies. Those available from the Reader's Digest, Lafayette Clinic, and the Life Education Program were not examined by the compiler. Those reprints available from a publisher that offer original pamphlet material on the subject as well are listed immediately after the originals. Otherwise, reprints are listed in a separate section further along in the bibliography. An exhaustive search for either government publications or reprints was not made.

Generally, this bibliography is selective only in that leads were followed from apparently reliable sources. Likely no one library will be interested in ordering the total lot. Therefore, certain items that the compiler feels will make a significant contribution to a vertical file collection have an asterisk by their entry number.

Consideration was given to arranging the entries by drug groups, e.g., stimulants, depressants, hallucinogens, narcotics, volatile substances, and general. However, a cursory examination of titles revealed that the vast majority of pamphlets fall into the general. Consequently, the decision was made to list all pamphlets under their respective publishers. This also facilitated compilation and will, it is hoped, expedite ordering.

GENERAL PUBLICATIONS

ADDICTION RESEARCH FOUNDATION
Communication Programs Division
33 Russell Street
Toronto 4, Ontario

1.   Fact Sheets, consisting of four pages each, are
        available from this Foundation on amphetamines,
barbiturates, cannabis, LSD, opiates, solvents, tranquilizers, and alcohol.   However, they will fill orders
consisting of NOT LESS THAN 10,000 COPIES OF ANY
ONE TITLE, $32.40 per thousand.
        Pamphlets are printed with the purchaser's
name and address, not ARF's, and the section dealing
with legal factors amended to coincide with the laws of
the region concerned.

ALLYN AND BACON, INC.
470 Atlantic Avenue
Boston, Massachusetts 02210

2.   Drugs and People.   1969.   44 p. $1.   5th and
        6th Grades.   By Donald A. Read, assistant
professor of health education, University of Massachusetts.   "Questions and answers" format with illustrations.   Spurs interest and written in understandable
terms.   Defines a drug, gives historical account of
their use, tells why people use drugs, how they can
help and hurt, the "how" of drug dependency, and the
law and drugs.   Accompanied by a "Teacher's Manual"
[see entry 3].

3.   Teachers' Manual for Drugs and People.   1969.
23 p.   36¢.   By same author as Drugs and
People.   Gives considerations for a drug education
program, chart on how to spot a user, glossary of
terms, resource materials for students and for teachers.
Lists pamphlets, articles, journals, books, and films.

AMERICAN ASSOCIATION FOR WORLD HEALTH, INC.
    777 United Nations Plaza
    New York, New York 10017

*4.   Drugs.   (April, 1971, issue of World Health
magazine.)   Superbly illustrated.   35 p.   50¢.
HS, Adults.   Surveys the world's drug scene.   Discusses what drugs do to us and explores reasons for
abusing them.   Suggests ways to treat and prevent the
problem.   Adequate inventories of this issue available
to fill probable nationwide demand.   Excellent.

AMERICAN COLLEGE HEALTH ASSOCIATION
    Regency Hyatt House
    Atlanta, Georgia

5.   Position Statement on Drug Abuse.   1970.   3
mimeographed pages.   SC free.   Adults.   In a
review of the legal, social, and pharmacological questions involved in the preoccupation of students and
faculty of many institutional communities with problems
related to inappropriate, unauthorized, or illegal use
of medications, the association has drafted this position paper.

AMERICAN EDUCATION PUBLICATIONS
    Education Center, Subscription Offices
    Columbus, Ohio 43216

*6.   Know About Drugs: A Guide for Students.   1969.
47 p.   illus.   40¢.   Grades 7-12.   Identifies and
gives effects of drugs.   Tells who uses and abuses, the
social problems involved, how good the cures are.   Human interest stories.   Valuable.

AMERICAN FEDERATION OF LABOR and CONGRESS
OF INDUSTRIAL ORGANIZATIONS
815 16th Street, N. W.
Washington, D. C. 20006

7.   What Every Worker Should Know About Drug
     Abuse. 1969. 5 p. 3¢. Concise and factual
discussion of the nation's drug problem, its characteristics and what unions can do to help their members
and the community at large.

THE AMERICAN LEGION
     National Commission on Children and Youth
     P. O. Box 1055
     Indianapolis, Indiana 46206

8.   The American Legion Statement of Policy on
     Drugs and Drug Abuse. 1971. 16 p. SC free.
Adults. A preamble gives an overview of the drug
problem and is followed by the "Fundamental Concept"
of the American Legion. Drug abuse as it relates to
international relations, education, the military, and the
veteran is covered, as well as the Legion's position on
marihuana. Their 38 major recommendations of policy
on drugs and drug abuse are stated along with 13 guidelines for Legion activity in the attack on drug abuse.
Recommended films and audiovisuals.

AMERICAN MEDICAL ASSOCIATION
     Order Department
     535 North Dearborn Street
     Chicago, Illinois 60610

9.   Amphetamines. (OP-197). 1970. 3 p. 10¢.
     HS, Adults. Discusses amphetamine abuse,
effects on abusers, and hazards of experimentation.

10. Barbiturates. (OP-196). 1970. 3 p. 10¢.
     HS, Adults. Defines them, tells how they are
used, why they are frequently involved in suicides,
and how they affect abusers.

11. The Crutch That Cripples--Drug Dependence. (OP-162). 1968. 17 p. 25¢. HS, Adults. Outlines the reasons for experimentation, the types of drugs which cause dependence, and the effects and symptoms of drug abuse.

12. Glue Sniffing. (OP-195). 1970. 3 p. 15¢. HS, Adults. Defines it, gives effects and hazards of experimentation.

13. LSD. (OP-194). 1970. 2 p. 10¢. HS, Adults. Describes the drug, tells how and why it is abused, and gives the hazards of experimentation, and legal controls.

14. Marihuana. (OP-198). 1970. 2 p. 10¢. HS, Adults. Its origins, effects, hazards, legal controls, and typical users.

Payment must accompany order on all the above; stamps not acceptable.

AMERICAN MEDICAL ASSOCIATION
   Department of Mental Health
   535 North Dearborn Street
   Chicago, Illinois 60610

15. Bibliography on Drug Abuse and Drug Dependence. 1969. 9 p. SC free. Includes magazine articles on drugs generally and on amphetamines, barbiturates, hallucinogens, narcotics, and solvents specifically.

16. A Marihuana (Cannabis) Bibliography. 1969. 5 p. SC free. Magazine articles on marihuana exclusively.

17. Selected Readings on Drug Abuse and Drug Dependence. 1970. 3 p. SC free. Covers books, booklets and pamphlets, magazine and newspaper articles.

JOURNAL OF THE AMERICAN MEDICAL ASSOCIA-
TION (JAMA) REPRINT SERVICE
   535 North Dearborn Street
   Chicago, Illinois 60610

18.   Dependence on Amphetamines and Other Stimu-
       lant Drugs. JAMA, 9-19-66, Vol. 197. 5 p.
Reprint. SC free. Adults.

19.   Dependence on Barbiturates and Other Sedative
       Drugs. JAMA, 8-23-65, Vol. 193. 5 p. Re-
print. SC free. Adults.

20.   Dependence on Cannabis (Marihuana). JAMA,
       8-7-67, Vol. 201. 4 p. Reprint. SC free.
Adults.

21.   Dependence on LSD and Other Hallucinogenic
       Drugs. JAMA, 10-2-67, Vol. 202. 4 p. Re-
print. SC free. Adults.

22.   Marihuana and Society. JAMA, 6-24-68, Vol.
       204. 2 p. Reprint. SC free. Adults.

23.   Marihuana Thing. JAMA, 6-24-68, Vol. 204.
       Broadside. Reprint. SC free. Adults.

AMERICAN NURSES' ASSOCIATION
   10 Columbus Circle
   New York, New York 10019

24.   Identification of Drug Addiction in Office and
       Industrial Settings. 1966. 12 p. 50¢. Adults.
Chapters cover the "spectrum" of addiction--five kinds
of addicts, recognizing the addict, and the nurse's re-
sponsibilities. Written by Susan D. Taylor, R. N.,
and publisher of magazine articles on drug addiction.

AMERICAN SOCIAL HEALTH ASSOCIATION
   1740 Broadway
   New York, New York 10019

*25.   Drug Abuse: A Call for Action. 1967. 32 p.
       50¢. Adults. Brief statement on topics dis-
cussed by 160 specialists at a National Community
Leadership Conference on Controlling Drug Abuse.
Texts of remarks made by Dr. Goulding and Dr. Eddy.

*26.   The Glue Sniffing Problem. n.d. 22 p. 20¢.
       Adults. By Charles Winick, Ph.D. and Jacob
Goldstein, Ph.D. An in-depth examination of the
causes of glue sniffing, effects, relation to drug dependence, extent of usage, possible remedies, etc.

*27.   A Guide to Some Drugs Which Are Subject to
       Abuse. 1971. Chart. 25¢. Defines drug
groups, gives slang names, tells how taken and how to
spot abuser, primary effects, and dangers.

*28.   The Narcotic Addiction Problem. 1968. 23 p.
       15¢. HS, Adults. Covers narcotic addiction
problem in the U.S. and a brief presentation of ASHA's
program.

*29.   Speed Kills: The Amphetamine Abuse Problem.
       1969. 22 p. 20¢. Jr. and Sr. HS, Adults.
Defines speed and speed high, tells how amphetamines
are manufactured and abused, and how adverse reactions are treated, and gives physical and psychological
effects, etc.

       ASHA publishes a curriculum guide for grades
kindergarten through high school entitled Teaching About
Drugs, $4: the first nationally produced illustrated
curriculum guide for the study of drug use and abuse.

THE AQUARIAN HOUSE
    425 Jackson Street
    Monterey, California 93940

30.   Basic Drug Facts: Some Straight Talk on Drugs.
       1970. 12 p. HS, Adults. Free. An excerpt
from A New Connection by John H. Frykman, former
director of the Drug Treatment Program of Haight-Ash-

bury Medical Clinic. Brief summary of drug families
and their relationships. Detailed information on PROJ-
ECT AQUARIUS is available upon request.

THE ARIZONA REPUBLIC
    City Editor
    120 East Van Buren Street
    Phoenix, Arizona

*31.   Youth and Drugs. 1970. 36 p. illus. Free
        "at this time." Adults. Written by a six-man
task force of reporters who talked with and questioned
users and abusers, addicts and ex-addicts, parents,
students, school officials, doctors, judges, attorneys,
law enforcement officers, sociologists, and community
leaders. Factual, informative.

ASSOCIATED PRESS
    Attention: Joe Wing
    50 Rockefeller Plaza
    New York, New York 10020

*32.   What You Can Do About Dangerous Drugs. 1971.
        Highly illustrated. 64 p. $1. By Alton Blake-
slee. Recommended by the deputy director of the Bureau of Narcotics and Dangerous Drugs not only for
parents and those interested in teaching drug respect,
but for young people who are subjected to the drug phe-
nomena in their everyday social contacts. Accurate
and factual.

*33.   What You Should Know About Drugs and Narcotics.
        1969. 48 p. Highly illustrated. $1. HS,
Adults. By Alton Blakeslee. Covers the drug scene
in America, the scope and signs of drug use, the major mind-affecting drugs, fuses of the mind-drug ex-
plosion, the appeal of drugs, the human price of mind
drugs, what parents can do, law and the "mind" drugs,
and the outlook for "mind" drugs. Excellent.

BELL TELEPHONE COMPANY
   Your Local Business Office

34.   According to Dr. Charles H. Rushmore, medical
      director of Indiana Bell, "there may be literally
hundreds of pamphlets used for drug abuse education
throughout the Bell System and there is no mechanism
for central indexing of such material." It is suggested
that local business offices of the Bell System be con-
tacted.

THE BENJAMIN COMPANY, INC.
   485 Madison Avenue
   New York, New York 10022

*35.   What You and Your Family Should Know About
       Drugs.   "Answers to the Most Frequently Asked
Questions About Drug Abuse." The official U.S. Government guide book. 1970. 50¢. HS, Adults. Pre-
face contains letter by Richard Nixon. Also printed in
Spanish: Lo que usted y su familia deben saber sobre
las drogas. Same price.

B'NAI B'RITH COMMISSION ON COMMUNITY AND
VETERANS SERVICES
   1640 Rhode Island Avenue, NW
   Washington, D.C. 20036

36.   I Didn't Know... An Adult Approach to Drug Abuse.
      n.d.   22 p.   50¢.   Adults.   Suggests means of
self and community education and action. Glossary of
slang terms. Selected references, films.

B'NAI B'RITH VOCATIONAL SERVICE
   1640 Rhode Island Avenue, NW
   Washington, D.C. 20036

37.   The Drug Abuser: A Challenge to the Counselor.
      1970.   Vol. 25, No. 4.   Special Supplement to
Counselor's Information Service.   11 p.   50¢.   Adults.

Published speech by Dr. Leonard G. Perlman.   Selected references and films.   Valuable insight.

B'NAI B'RITH YOUTH ORGANIZATION
   1640 Rhode Island Avenue, NW
   Washington, D. C. 20036

38.   Drug Abuse--Advisor Supplement (ADV-41).   n. d.
      10¢.   Adults.   Addressed to the adult worker,
professional or volunteer with youth groups.   Tells
how to deal with teenage experimentation and drug
abuse.   To be used with the following pamphlets.

39.   Drugs Are Not the Problem (PG-26).   1970.
      23 p.   25¢.   Adults.   Deals primarily but not
exclusively with marihuana.   Concerned with drugs as
a symptom of more general problems of teenagers
growing up and suggests ways to deal with the basic
problem rather than the symptoms.

40.   Drugs Are Still Not the Problem... But... (ADV-
      43).   1970.   7 p.   10¢.   Adults.   Deals with
drug abuse as an increasingly acceptable teenage fad,
affecting "normal" and troubled youngsters alike.   Suggests ways of directing the trend.

BUDLONG PRESS COMPANY
   5428 N. Virginia Avenue
   Chicago, Illinois 60625

*41.   A Doctor Discusses Narcotics and Drug Addiction.
       1969.   illus.   90 p. $1.75.   HS, Adults.   Cov-
ers drug dependence, drug group information, encoun-
ters with drug users--depicting how and why they got
started--the addict's need for help and the need to find
a better way out of Drugville.   By Louis Relin in consultation with Robert L. Sharoff, M. D.   Very good.

BUTLER UNIVERSITY
   College of Pharmacy
   Indianapolis, Indiana 46208

42.   Drug Abuse: A Course for Educators; A Report
       of the Butler University Drug Abuse Institute.
1968.   157 p. $2.   Adults.   Prefaced by chairman
of the National Coordinating Council on Drug Abuse Education and Information.   Topics discussed by impres-
sive list of personages.   Comprehensive coverage.

43.   Today's Drugs of Abuse.   n. d.   8 mimeographed
       sheets.   SC free.   Adults.   By K. L. Kaufman,
dean of the College of Pharmacy, Butler University and
Dr. O. L. Salerni, associate professor of Medicinal
Chemistry.   "One of many talks that various faculty
members have presented to hundreds of different audi-
ences."

CALIFORNIA MEDICAL ASSOCIATION
    Division of Scientific and Educational Activities
    693 Sutter Street
    San Francisco, California 94102

44.   LSD Fact Sheet.   n. d.   Broadside.   Free.   HS,
       Adults.

45.   Speed Fact Sheet.   n. d.   Broadside.   Free.   HS,
       Adults.

46.   Straight Dope About Heroin.   Health Tips, June,
       1970.   2 p.   Free.

47.   Damaging Effects of Drug Abuse.   1969.   8 p.
       Reprint.   Free.   HS, Adults.   Questions and
answers concerning drugs and drug abuse.   Reprinted
from the San Francisco Examiner, Health Forum Series.   Concise.

48.   Marijuana: Social Benefit or Social Detriment.
       11 mimeographed pages.   Reprint from California
Medicine, 106:346-353, May, 1967.   By E. R. Bloom-
quist, M. D.   Free.   Available from the Committee on
Dangerous Drugs, California Medical Association, 1910
Niodrara Drive, Glendale, California 91208

CALIFORNIA STATE DEPARTMENT OF EDUCATION
    721 Capitol Mall
    Sacramento, California 95814

*49.   Drug Abuse: A Source Book and Guide for
        Teachers. 1967. 131 p. 40¢. Foreword by
Max Rafferty, superintendent of public instruction. Besides education's role and guiding principles for an instructional program, provides general information about
dangerous drugs, volatile chemicals, legal controls,
etc.

CHANNING L. BETE CO., INC.
    45 Federal Street
    Greenfield, Massachusetts 01301

50.   Drugs and You. 1969. 15 p. Cartoon-illus.
       25¢. Elem., HS. Gives medical use and dan-
gers of abuse of various drugs, legal controls and penalties. Valuable.

51.   What Everyone Should Know About Drug Abuse.
       1971. 15 p. Cartoon-illus. 25¢. Elem., H.S.
Covers basic social aspects of drug abuse. Valuable.

52.   The Bete Co. also publishes a Drug Information
       Center, each compact unit containing 100 copies
of eight different fact folders on the following abused
drugs: marihuana, heroin, barbiturates, hallucinogens,
amphetamines, deliriants, opiates, and cocaine. The
eight fact folders are available only in packets of 100
or as a part of the complete display unit (with the exception of the samples sent for purchase consideration).
One to nine complete units cost $51 each; ten to 29
units cost $47 each.

THE CHRISTOPHERS
    12 E. 48th Street
    New York, New York 10017

53.   Christopher News Notes No. 178. n.d. 12-page

folder. SC free. Available in quantity of 100
for $1 and 1,000 for $9. HS, Adults. An overview
of the problem and what is being done through legal,
educational and rehabilitation channels. A chart of primary effects and dangers of drug abuse.

CHRONICLE GUIDANCE PUBLICATIONS, INC.
Moravia, New York 13118

54.   Drug Abuse and You. 1968. School edition 24 p.
       50¢; Trade edition 32 p. 75¢. HS, Adults.
Chapters include substances of abuse and their effects,
explanation of terms, the widely abused drugs, why
drug abuse, and a chart of primary substances which
may be abused. Written by the dean and the assistant
dean of students at California State College, and a free-
lance writer. Suggested readings. Objective.

55.   WHY? Poster chart. Lists primary substances
       which may be abused. 75¢. Quantity rates.

56.   Drug Use Among the Young. 8 p. Reprint. 50¢.

57.   Leaving the Drug World Behind. 4 p. Reprint.
       35¢.

58.   Marijuana & LSD--A Reading for Counselors.
       8 p. Reprint. 50¢.

59.   Reversing the Dehumanizing Process as a Means
       of Combating Drug Abuse. 4 p. Reprint. 35¢.

       Quantity rates available on request.

CLARETIAN PUBLICATIONS
   221 W. Madison Street
   Chicago, Illinois 60606

60.   Drugs Today. 1970. 71 p. illus. 75¢. HS,
       Adults. Includes brief history of how the phar-

macological age was born, reasons for youth's drug
involvement, definition of the various drug groups,
physical effects and what drugs may offer mankind in
the future. Drug cult glossary.

61. Mind-Expanding Drugs. 1967. 23 p. 15¢.
     Adults. A report on the effects and future impli-
cations of LSD and other controversial mind-expanding
drugs.

COMMUNITY SERVICE SOCIETY
     105 East 22 Street
     New York, New York 10010

62. Marihuana: The Non-Narcotic Dangerous Drug.
     1970. 15 p. Free. Adults. Four papers ex-
amining the need for reclassification and for changes
in penalties.

63. Reclassification of Marihuana as a Non-Narcotic
     Dangerous Drug. 1970. 10 p. Free. Adults.
Position paper summarizing the arguments for reclassification of marihuana as a non-narcotic dangerous
drug and for changes in the penalties so that they are
related to the actual hazards of the drug.

DO IT NOW FOUNDATION
     Box 3573
     Hollywood, California 90028

64. Amphetamine Abuse: Pattern and Effects of High
     Doses Taken Intravenously. n. d. 6-page folder.
10¢. HS, Adults.

65. Communications Techniques for Parents. n. d.
     4 p. 10¢. Adults.

66. The Comic Book: Primary Supplement to Do It
     Now Educational Program. 8 p. 15¢. Ages 8-
     12.

67. Conscientious Guide to Drug Abuse. n. d. 40 p.
     $1. HS, Adults. Takes a comprehensive look
at street drugs. Written entirely on an underground
level. Necessary information for anyone who must
counsel or work in an intensive street drug environment.

68. Drug IQ Test. n. d. 6-page folder. 15¢. HS,
     Adults.

69. The Facts About Downers. n. d. 6-page folder.
     10¢. Jr. and Sr. HS.

70. Introduction to In-School Drug Education. n. d.
     6-page folder. 10¢. Educators.

71. A 19-Year Old Girl and Poet Allen Ginsberg Talk
     About Speed. n. d. 6-page folder. 10¢. HS,
     Adults.

72. SMACK: The Strongest Thing You Can Buy With-
     out a Prescription. n. d. 6-page folder. 10¢.
HS, Adults.

73. The Sniffing Spectrum. n. d. 6-page folder.
     10¢. HS, Adults.

74. Vibrations Newspaper. n. d. 8-page tabloid con-
     taining peer-group facts and news about drugs.
Highly illustrated. 15¢. HS, Adults.

     A price list is available from the Foundation.

DRUG ADDICTION REHABILITATION ENTERPRISE
(DARE)
     211 Littleton Avenue
     Newark, New Jersey 07103

75. Dare: A Direction to a New Way of Life. n. d.
     10 p. Free. Adults. Explains DARE's pro-
grams for rehabilitation, prevention, education, and research. A New Jersey enterprise recommended by the
chairman of the Narcotic Drug Study Commission.

EDUCATIONAL AIDS OF LONG BEACH
  P.O. Box 4242
  Long Beach, California 90804

76. Fact Book: A Drug Abuse Manual.   (No. 352).
     1970.   23 p.   illus.   15¢.   Recommended for
teachers, parents, law enforcement agencies, armed
services, public health offices, service groups and other civic minded groups.   Besides basic drug data, information is given on how to spot a user and what to
do.   Projects and discussions are suggested.   There
are two case histories, drug slang, and a sample ques-
tionnaire.

77. "Users are Losers!" What You Should Know
     About Drug Abuse!   (No. 350).   1970.   16 p.
4-color fully illustrated.   Samples on request.   Elementary grades through high school.   A logical appeal
to youngsters.   Pamphlet has received endorsement by
many educators and other authorities.   Available also
from The Order of the Golden Rule (q.v.).

     Educational Aids has available a brochure of their
publications, listing an identification chart, "kickee
stickees," displays, marihuana plant facsimiles, marihuana odor tablets, etc.

EDUCATIONAL SUMMARIES, INC.
  P.O. Bin No. 14
  Pasadena, California 91109

*78. Diseases and Disorders That May Result from
      Drug Abuse.   1971.   8 p.   Highly illus.   50¢.
HS, Adults.   Maladies listed by drug groups.   Summary on last page.   Good.

*79. Stop the "Street Market" Suppliers.   1971.   8 p.
      Highly illus.   50¢.   HS, Adults.   Tells how the
drugs get there and who makes the huge profits from
their ultimate sale to youth.   Pointers for a crash
campaign to stop suppliers.   Good.

*80.   A Summary for Parents and Students on a Sub-
        ject of Teenage Drug Abuse. 1969. 8 p. Highly
illus.   50¢. HS, Adults. Pills and capsules laid out,
giving symptoms of their overuse. Good.

ELI LILLY AND COMPANY [Manufacturer of Pharmaceutical Products]
    307 East McCarty Street
    Indianapolis, Indiana 46206

81.   Drug Abuse, Drug Dependence. 1969. 4-page
        folder. Available free for classroom use. HS,
Adults.   Article is reproduced from a news release by
the American Medical Association.

82.   Drug Abuse: What One Company Is Doing About
        It. n.d. 4 p. Free. Questions and answers.
Includes an excellent composite statement taken from a
Fortune article (January, 1969) which is based on opin-
ions expressed by 200 students on a score of campuses.
Pamphlet explains the major responsibility of the phar-
maceutical industry in the drug dilemma.

GENERAL TELEPHONE & ELECTRONICS CORPORA-
TION
    730 Third Avenue
    New York, New York 10017

83.   Drug Abuse and Misuse. n.d. 21 p. Free.
        HS, Adults. Defines drugs that are most com-
monly misused, describes their uses, abuses, and effects, and lists the common symptoms they produce.
Valuable.

GEORGIA DEPARTMENT OF EDUCATION
    Curriculum Development Division
    Office of Instructional Services
    Atlanta, Georgia 30434

*84.   Viewpoints: Drug Use, Misuse and Abuse. 1970.

36 p.   50¢.   Check or money order; no stamps.
Primarily an information source with some suggestions
for teaching.   Provides guidance and lists materials
for instruction in elementary and secondary school.
Federal controls given.

GOOD READING RACK SERVICE
    P. O. Box 450
    Stamford, Connecticut 06904

85.   The Dangers of Drug Misuse.   1970.   14 p.
    illus.   35¢.   HS, Adults.   Good general informa-
tion on the various drug groups and where an addict
can go to get help.

GUIDANCE ASSOCIATES [A subsidiary of Harcourt
Brace Jovanovich, Inc.]
    41 Washington Avenue
    Pleasantville, New York 10570

*86.   Drugs: The Unsuspected Intruder; a Guide for
       Community Leaders and Parents.   1970.   32 p.
    $1.   illus.   Adults.   Surveys the drug problem, tells
why it exists, stresses the need for a massive training
program for adults, discusses the role of law enforcement, gives symptoms of various drug abusers, treatment and rehabilitation, and glossary of terms.   Booklet is included with two sound filmstrips but may be
ordered separately.   Written in depth.   Excellent.

KIWANIS INTERNATIONAL
    101 East Erie Street
    Chicago, Illinois 60611

87.   Deciding About Drugs.   1969.   14 p.   illus.
    Upper elementary or Jr. HS.   SC free.   Basic
information on the most frequently abused drugs and
their effects.   Appeals to a rational decision by youth.

88.   What If They Call Me Chicken.   1970.   16 p.

Comic book.   SC free.   10, 11, 12-year old children.   A young boy under pressure to use drugs discusses his problem with his father and college-student
brother.

Bibliographies:

89.   Booklets, Brochures, and Pamphlets Designed
      for Mass Distribution to Children and Adults.
(ODA-12).   6 p.   SC free.

90.   Books Suggested for Public Library Purchase.
      (ODA-14).   3 p.   SC free.

91.   Films, Filmstrips, Tapes and Other Audio-Visual
      Materials.   (ODA-10).   12 p.   SC free.

92.   Materials Available from U.S. Government Agen-
      cies.   (ODA-9).   5 p.   SC free.

92a. Materials for Reference and Background Study.
      (ODA-13).   6 p.   SC free.

93.   Posters, Charts, Buttons, Decals, etc.   (ODA-
      11).   2 p.   SC free.

94.   Resources for Classroom Use.   (ODA-15).   5 p.
      SC free.

The above bibliographies were primarily prepared
for use by local Kiwanis Clubs.   They are excellent.

METROPOLITAN LIFE INSURANCE COMPANY
    One Madison Avenue
    New York, New York 10010

*95. To Parents/About Drugs.   1970.   20 p.   Free.
      Adults.   Basic information about drugs, the need
for controls and preventions, how parents can tell if
children abuse drugs, and finding help.   Drug chart included.   Very good.

*96.   To Young Teens on Druggism.   1971.   6 p.
        Free.   HS, Adults.   Logical appeal to reader.
Excellent.

NARCOTIC ADDICTION CONTROL COMMISSION
    State of New York
    Executive Park South
    Albany, New York 12203

    [Free distribution is limited out-of-state to single
copies of a number of excellent bibliographies, brochures, reports, and reprints as listed below.]

*97.   Amphetamines--the Stimulant Drugs.   n.d.   6-
        page folder.   HS, Adults.

*98.   Annotated Bibliography of Literature on Narcotic
        Addiction.   1968.   76 p.   Adults.   Abstracts al-
most 150 books and articles.   Literature reviewed is
divided in 12 categories such as definition of addiction,
characteristics of addicts, treatment, and rehabilitation
programs, etc.   Index.

*99.   Barbiturates--the Depressant Drugs.   n.d.   6-
        page folder.   HS, Adults.

*100.   Cocaine.   n.d.   8-page folder.   HS, Adults.

*101.   Deliriants.   n.d.   6-page folder.   HS, Adults.
        Names deliriants, gives death statistics, effects,
and dependence.

*102.   The Drug Problem--New York State's Total Ap-
        proach: Prevention, Treatment, Research.   n.d.
8-page folder.   Adults.

*103.   Drugs: A Pocket Primer.   n.d.   A chart giving
        classification, medical use, popular types, nick-
names, how taken, effects, dependence, tolerance,
physical complications, and comments on drug groups.
HS, Adults.

*104. For Your Information: A Methadone Primer.
      n.d.   6-page folder. HS, Adults.

*105. A Handbook of Drug Terms. Revised, 1971.
      17 p. HS, Adults. Glossary of drug terms. In-
cludes the jargons of the street and of the laboratory.

*106. Help a Narcotic Addict. . . n.d. 4 p. Adult.
      Tells how an addict enters New York State's re-
habilitation program, also questions and answers.

*107. Heroin--The Crutch. n.d. 6-page folder. HS,
      Adults. Gives derivation of the word heroin and
heroin itself, history of its use, public response to its
use.

*108. Marijuana. n.d. 6-page folder. HS, Adults.

*109. LSD. n.d. 6-page folder. HS, Adults.

*110. LSD, Pot Compared. n.d. 6-page folder. HS,
      Adults.

*111. New York State Revised Penal Law 9/69--Penal-
      ties for Sale or Possession of Narcotics. (Arti-
cle 220--Dangerous Drug Offenses). 6 p. Adults.

*112. New York's Fight Against Drug Abuse. 1969 An-
      nual Report and Supplement. 25 p. Adults.
Gives highlights of programs, administration, treatment,
prevention, research, personnel, new projects, budget,
and a statistical summary.

*113. Questions and Answers on Barbiturates, Ampheta-
      mines, LSD, Marijuana, Narcotics. n.d. 8-
page folder. HS, Adults.

*114. Second Annual Statistical Report of the Narcotic
      Addiction Control Commission for the year ending
3-31-69. 148 p. Adults. Contains information that
has been derived from data submitted by treatment fa-
cilities, accredited agencies, and centers for medical
examinations.

*115. Suggested Starting Bibliography in Narcotic Educa-
       tion. 1969. 5 p. By H. Brill, M.D. Includes
paperbacks, WHO Reports, books, government reports.

*116. Cool Talk About Hot Drugs. n.d.   8 p.   By
       Donald B. Louria, M.D. Reprinted by permis-
sion of the New York Times Company. HS, Adults.

*117. An Expert Answers Teen-Agers' Questions About
       Drugs. n.d. 6-page folder. By Stanley Yolles,
M.D. Reprinted by permission of Family Weekly Magazine. HS, Adults. Six guidelines for parents included.

*118. Problems of Inpatient Treatment of Addiction.
       n.d. 12 p. By Warren P. Jurgensen, M.D.
Reprinted from The International Journal of the Addic-
tions. Adults.

*119. A Psychiatrist Asks Why. n.d. Broadside on
       drugs. Reprinted by permission of Teen. HS,
Adults.

*120. The Relapse Rate in Narcotic Addiction: A Cri-
       tique of Follow-Up Studies. n.d. 21 p. By
John A. O'Donnell. Reprinted by permission of Mc-
Graw-Hill, 1965.

*121. Some Considerations in the Treatment of Non-
       Narcotic Drug Abusers. n.d. 24 p. By Carl
D. Chambers, Ph.D. and Leon Brill, MSW. Reprinted
by permission from Industrial Medicine and Surgery,
January, 1971. Adults.

*122. The Use of Drugs by Teenagers for Sanctuary and
       Illusion. n.d. 9 p. By Norman J. Levy, M.D.
Reprinted from The American Journal of Psychoanaly-
sis, Vol. XXVIII, 1. Adults.

*123. Why Intelligent Young People Take Drugs. n.d.
       8 p. Reprint. By Graham B. Blaine, Jr.,
M.D., chief of psychiatry, Harvard University. A

lecture given by Dr. Blaine in 1968 at an annual meeting of the Iowa Medical Society. Adults.

NARCOTIC EDUCATIONAL FOUNDATION OF AMERICA
   5055 Sunset Boulevard
   Los Angeles, California 90027

    Single copies of the following items, some of which are reprints, are available free. The Foundation publishes a price list for quantity lots and solicits assistance to reimburse costs for free materials.

124. Drug Addiction. n. d. 2 p. HS, Adults. Discusses drug dependence, effects of various drugs.

125. The Drug Problem--a Growing Abuse. n. d. 2-page leaflet. HS, Adults. Used by permission of U. S. Department of Health, Education, and Welfare.

126. Drugs and Alcohol. n. d. 4 p. HS, Adults. By Eugene F. Carey, M. D. , Department of Police, Chicago.

127. Drugs and Our Automotive Age. n. d. 6-page folder. HS, Adults. Prepared by U. S. Department of Health, Education, and Welfare.

128. A Marijuana "Test Case" in the Courts. 1968. Student Reference Sheet. HS, Adults.

129. Facts About Marijuana. n. d. 9 p. HS, Adults. By the Los Angeles Police Department. Covers all aspects of the drug.

130. LSD: Questions and Answers. n. d. 10 p. HS, Adults. By the Los Angeles Police Department. Covers entire spectrum of the drug.

131. Living Death. n. d. 4 p. HS, Adults. By U. S. Bureau of Narcotics. Deals mainly with the physical effects of drug addiction and tells how not to start.

132. Marihuana and Crime. 1966. 8 p. By James
     C. Munch, Ph. D. Cites specific cases of crimes
in the U. S. after use, and under influence, of marihuana. Based on a speech before the International Narcotic Enforcement Officers Association, 1965. Adults.

133. Questions and Answers: Barbiturates, Ampheta-
     mines, LSD, Marijuana, Narcotics. n. d. 12 p.
HS, Adults.

134. There Is a Difference! Marijuana vs. Alcohol.
     n. d. Broadside. HS, Adults.

135. The U. N. Reports on Marijuana Dangers Reveal-
     ing: "From every point of view, whether phys-
ical, mental, social or criminological." (UN document
E /CN. 7 /L. 91). n. d. Student Reference Sheet. HS,
Adults. Covers medical use and harmful effects.

136. Why Emphasize the Mildness of a Drug That Is
     Not Altogether Mild? n. d. Student Reference
Sheet. HS, Adults.

137. Youth and Narcotics: A Study of Juvenile Drug
     Addiction. n. d. 6-page folder. HS, Adults.
Cites an average case, discusses aspects and contagion
of addiction, and how to recognize the juvenile addict.

138. Glue Sniffing. n. d. 6-page folder. Reprint.
     HS, Adults. Excerpts from Listen magazine and
Western Medicine.

139. A Growing Menace--Drug Addiction. n. d. 6-
     page folder. HS, Adults. By Harris Isbell,
M. D., head of the U. S. Public Health Hospital, Lexington, Kentucky. Reprinted from The Merck Report.

140. Marijuana: Social Benefit or Social Detriment?
     1967. 8 p. Adults. Written by Edward R.
Bloomquist, M. D.; reprinted from California Medicine.
See also California Medical Association.

141. Study Finds Frequent Marijuana Smoking Is Harm-
     ful to Youth. 1971. 2-page leaflet. HS, Adults.
Five-year survey by two doctors shows serious psycho-
logical effects can be produced. Reprinted from Wall
Street Journal, 4-19-71.

NATIONAL ASSOCIATION OF BLUE SHIELD PLANS
     211 East Chicago Avenue
     Chicago, Illinois 60611

*142. Drug Abuse: The Chemical Cop-Out. 1969.
      illus. 44 p. SC free. Adults. Available from
local Blue Shield Plans or the National Association.
Endorsed by Art Linkletter and John Finlator, associate
director of the Federal Bureau of Narcotics and Dangerous Drugs. Basic information. Also takes look at
the users and examines some of the factors which may
be contributing to increased drug abuse. Excellent.

NATIONAL ASSOCIATION OF CHAIN DRUG STORES,
INC.
     1911 Jefferson Davis Highway
     Arlington, Virginia 22202

143. Stop Drug Abuse. n.d. 6 p. SC free. HS,
     Adults. Provides a listing of general symptoms,
charts, and pamphlet and film sources of drug abuse
education information.

NATIONAL CLEARINGHOUSE FOR DRUG ABUSE IN-
FORMATION (NCDAI)
     5454 Wisconsin Avenue
     Chevy Chase, Maryland 20515

     (The NCDAI, operated by the National Institute of
Mental Health on behalf of the federal agencies engaged
in drug abuse education programs, is the focal point
for federal information on drug abuse.)

*144. A Federal Source Book: Answers to the Most

Frequently Asked Questions About Drug Abuse.
1971. 30 p. HS, Adults. SC free. Based on the
latest research findings of the National Institute of
Mental Health in cooperation with other federal agencies and departments concerned with drug abuse. Also
available from the U. S. Superintendent of Documents
for 25¢, Catalog No. PREX 13. 2:An8. Revised frequently.

*145. Selected Drug Education Curricula Series. Se-
lected curricula reprinted with the permission of
the originating school system, eight in number. Single
courtesy copies are available from the NCDAI. A
"Resource Book for Drug Abuse Education" is recommended to be used in conjunction with the curricula.
It is available from the U. S. Superintendent of Documents (Catalog No. FS2. 22:D84/12, PHS Pub. 1964)
or National Education Association.

THE NATIONAL COORDINATING COUNCIL ON DRUG
ABUSE EDUCATION AND INFORMATION, INC.
  Suite 212, 1211 Connecticut Ave., N. W.
  Washington, D. C. 20036

(The Council is a private, non-profit organization
working to combat drug abuse through education and information. Its membership includes more than 97 national governmental, professional, educational, law enforcement, service, religious, and youth organizations.
In addition, the Council is extending affiliation membership to regional, state and local groups and organizations working in the area of drug abuse education and
information.)

146. Common Sense Lives Here: A Community Guide
to Drug Abuse Action. 1970. 96 p. illus. $2.
Adults. Step-by-step guide to community drug abuse
organization. Includes chapters on basic facts about
drugs, organizing your community for action and where
to find help. Practical and specific suggestions. Glossary of drug abuse terms.

147. Directory. 1970. 90 p. $1. Adults. Compila-
     tion of information about the National Coordinating
Council's members and affiliates including valuable
facts regarding their publications, films, services,
meetings, and whom to contact and where.

148. Marihuana and Health: Introduction and Summary
     of a Report to the Congress. 1971. 10 p. 25¢.
Adults. A report from the Secretary of Health, Education and Welfare. Covers subjective effects, acute
physiological effects of marihuana use, acute psychotic
episodes, intellectual and motor performance, marihuana and birth defects, effects of long-term chronic use,
marihuana and the use of other drugs, and future research directions.

     The Council furnishes a list of publications avail-
able from them on the subject of drug education.

NATIONAL COUNCIL OF CHURCHES
     Department of Ministry
     475 Riverside Drive
     New York, New York 10027

149. The Pastor and Drug Dependency. 1968. 23 p.
     50¢. Adults. By Howard J. Clinebell, Jr., pro-
fessor of pastoral counseling, School of Theology at
Claremont, California. Covers the problem, the drugs,
legislative controls, dependency and factors fostering
it, the broader challenge in the imminent flowering of
the "age of psychochemistry," and pastoral care of
drug-dependent persons.

NATIONAL DISTRICT ATTORNEYS' ASSOCIATION
     211 East Chicago Avenue
     Chicago, Illinois 60611

*150. Developing a Prosecutor's Program to Combat
      Drug Abuse Among Young People. 1968. 61 p.
 $2. HS, Adults. Surveys the drug problem in the
 U.S., discusses the expansion of the prosecutor's role

in deterring drug abuse, gives alternative approaches
in education and information, and guidelines for devel-
opment of a prosecutor's program in his own community. Also describes the DEANS--a select group of
young people who are leaders in their respective schools
and peer groups and who are interested in becoming
well informed on the problem of drug abuse and serving
as allies in the war against it. Excellent.

NATIONAL EDUCATION ASSOCIATION
    Publication-Sales Section
    1201 Sixteenth Street, N.W.
    Washington, D.C. 20036

*151. Drug Abuse: A Primer for Parents. n.d. 8-page
       folder. SC free. Additional copies available at
30 for $1. Orders must be prepaid. Order from
American Education Week, P.O. Box 327, Hyattsville,
Maryland 20781

*152. Drug Abuse: Escape to Nowhere; a Guide for
       Educators. Revised, 1970. 104 p. illus. $2.
Originally published for educators, this factual, en-
lightening look into the complex world of drug abuse
can be used effectively by parents. Written in non-
technical terms, the book explores the history of drug
abuse, the effects of the drugs most commonly abused,
and way in which youngsters can be reached. An information resource, not a plan for teaching. Technical
definitions and glossary of slang terms. Drug chart.
Selected films, books, pamphlets, and articles. Excellent.

*153. Resource Book for Drug Abuse Education. n.d.
       117 p. $1.25. Teachers. Contains summaries
of factual information on the major drugs of abuse, and
techniques and suggestions that experienced drug educators have found helpful in communicating with young
people who are thinking about drugs or have already ex-
perimented with them. Includes range of views by
medical authorities and social scientists. Section on
planning drug abuse education workshops. Selected ref-

erences.   Available also from Superintendent of Documents, $1.25.   Excellent.

*154. How Can We Teach Adolescents About Smoking,
        Drinking, and Drug Abuse? 1968.   6 p.   30¢.
Educators.   Reprinted from the Journal of HPER.

THE NATIONAL FOUNDATION
    March of Dimes
    800 Second Avenue
    New York, New York 10017
        Orders to: The National Foundation
        P.O. Box 2000, White Plains, New York 10602

155. Don't Get Hooked on "Harmless Drugs!" n.d.   4-
       page leaflet.   Free.   Advice to expectant mothers.

156. Drugs and Birth Defects.   n.d.   2 p.   Free.
       Adults.

157. It's Possible! Birth Defects Prevention.   n.d.
        9 p.   Free.   One page is devoted to unprescribed
drugs.

NEW JERSEY DEPARTMENT OF EDUCATION
    225 West State Street
    P.O. Box 2019
    Trenton, New Jersey 08625

*158. Drug Abuse: A Reference for Teachers.   1969.
        71 p.   50¢.   Information source covering entire
drug abuse spectrum with a bibliography, list of films,
information sources, and a glossary of terms.   Included is a chapter on the role of the school and a
chapter on the instructional program.   Very good. Suggested Education Teaching Units, Grades k-12, is also
available: the compiler was sent a sample copy, but
no price was given.

NEW JERSEY STATE LAW ENFORCEMENT PLANNING
AGENCY
    447 Bellevue Avenue
    Trenton, New Jersey 08618

159. Drug Abuse and Crime in New Jersey: A Uni-
    form Crime Reporting Survey Conducted by the
Division of State Police. (Dissemination Document No.
10.) 1971. 49 p. No price given. Publication is intended to serve as a factual indicator of the relation-
ship between drug abuse and crime within the limits of
the data collected. Basic tenet of study is to measure
that which is measurable as it relates to the known
drug abuser and his total criminal involvement. Charts
and graphs.

NEW YORK CHAMBER OF COMMERCE
    65 Liberty Street
    New York, New York 10005

160. Drug Abuse as a Business Problem: The Prob-
    lem Defined with Guidelines for Policy. 1971.
64 p. $2. Adults. A booklet of guidelines primarily
intended for business firms in the New York area, although may prove useful elsewhere. Based on extensive interviews with a wide cross-section of officers
and medical executives from over 30 leading American
companies and written by Carol Kurtis, editor of the
Research Institute of America. Prefaced by Governor
Nelson A. Rockefeller.

NEWSWEEK
    Director, Responsibility Series
    444 Madison Avenue
    New York, New York 10022

161. Ten Facts Parents Should Know About Marijuana.
    n.d. Colorful broadside. 500 copies gratis.
HS, Adults. Gives the what, the where, the who, the
how of marihuana. Also dependence characteristics,
link to narcotics, and penalties for use and possession.

NEYENESCH PRINTERS, INC.
   2750 Kettner Boulevard
   P. O. Box 430
   San Diego, California 92112

*162. No Secret: A Compilation of Information on Nar-
       cotics and Dangerous Drugs. 1967. 14 p. 10¢.
HS, Adults. A condensed presentation, for student use,
of basic facts about drugs commonly abused. Contains
a section designed to alert students to the legal consequences of drug abuse and another which invites students to consider, prior to making a decision, a dozen
possible consequences of drug abuse. Very good.
[Published by permission of San Diego City Schools.]

NORTH CONWAY INSTITUTE, INC.
   8 Newbury Street
   Boston, Massachusetts 02116

163. Time for a Change--Attitudes on Alcohol and
      Drugs. 1970. 32 p. $2.50. Adults. Con-
densed and organized publication of discussions in 1969
by national leaders in fields of alcohol and drug problems at North Conway Institute, an ecumenical organization concerned with the prevention of problem drinking and drug dependence.

164. What You Need to Know About Drugs. n.d. 6-page
      flyer. 10¢. HS, Adults. Also available from
United Methodist Board of Christian Social Concerns.

OFFICE OF THE ATTORNEY GENERAL
   Rm. 1, State House Annex
   Columbus, Ohio 43215

165. AG Hits Drug Abuse. 1971. 4 p. A free news-
      letter. Adults. Tells of Ohio's all-out effort to
rid the state of the ills of drug abuse. One page de-
voted to drug groups.

OFFICE OF THE DISTRICT ATTORNEY
    600 Hall of Justice
    211 West Temple Street
    Los Angeles, California 90012

166. District Attorney's Young Citizens Council Speak-
      ers Manual. n.d. 56 p. SC free. A collection
of magazine reprints, excerpts, articles, and testimo-
nies concerning drug abuse. One chapter covers what
can be done, how it starts, how parents can help, danger signs, and the addict's lingo. Final chapter gives
some speech tips and a bibliography. [No longer available from the source.]

THE ORDER OF THE GOLDEN RULE [An International
Affiliation of Dependable Funeral Directors]
    726 South College Street
    Springfield, Illinois 62704

167. "Users are Losers!" 1970. 16 p. SC free.
      Elem, HS. Cartoon-like presentation. Covers
whole drug scene. Written in cooperation with police,
medical, pharmaceutical, educational and government
authorities. Also available from Educational Aids of
Long Beach.

168. The Word is Hooked: Plain Facts About Teen-
      Age Drug Addiction. 1968. 15 p. SC free.
HS, College. Good general information, covering four
categories of drugs and what a student can do when he
becomes hooked.

PACIFIC PRESS PUBLISHING ASSOCIATION
    1350 Villa Street
    Mountain View, California 94040

169. Pot Luck: What It's Like to Turn Yourself Off
      by Turning On with Drugs. 1970. 63 p. illus.
40¢. HS. Collection of teen-age stories reprinted
from magazines, and an article by Dr. Lindsay R.
Curtis on marihuana.

PARENTS' LEAGUE OF HOUSTON
    Post Office Box 22733
    Houston, Texas 77027

*170. Youth and Drugs: A Handbook for Parents. 1969.
    75 p. illus. 35¢. Adults. Chapters include
points for parents; a Houston survey of young people
between the ages of 12 and 21; descriptions, sources,
and effects of drugs; how to tell if a youngster is ex-
perimenting; legal consequences; psychological facts;
how the schools can help; where to seek help in Houston. Pamphlet is being revised. Price increase certain.

PENNSYLVANIA, COMMONWEALTH OF
    Division of Public Health Education
    Division of Drug Control
    Department of Health
    Harrisburg, Pennsylvania

171. Teachers' Resource Guide on Drug Abuse. 1969.
    155 p. Primarily for use of instructors. $1.
Nine concepts concerning drugs and their abuse are
contained in Part I. Part II is for the instructor's
general use. Appendices cover addresses of information sources, an annotated bibliography of books and
booklets, and a glossary of technical and slang terms.
A guide, not a text. Very good.

PHARMACEUTICAL MANUFACTURERS ASSOCIATION
    1155 Fifteenth Street, N. W.
    Washington, D. C. 20005

172. Drug Abuse Products Reference Chart. n. d.
    Folder. HS, Adults. Free up to 200 copies.
Slang and chemical name given for each drug, as well
as source, medical use, how taken when abused, long-
term possible effects, Federal control, etc.

173. Identification of Drug Abusers. n. d. 3-page fold-
    er. HS, Adults. Free up to 200 copies. Gives

symptoms experienced by the depressant, stimulant, narcotic, marihuana, and LSD abusers, as well as the glue sniffer.

174. The Medicines Your Doctor Prescribes: A Guide for Consumers. n.d. 9 p. illus. HS, Adults. Free up to 50 copies. Does not deal directly with drug abuse but provides information to guard against unintentional abuse of medicines.

175. The Problem of Drug Abuse. n.d. 13 p. Free. HS, Adults. Cites tragic effects of drug abuse, gives reasons for abuse, tells how various drugs when abused affect the user, and the importance of finding solutions. Not slanted. Logical. (Color slides are available to illustrate this presentation at a cost of $15.)

PHILIPS ROXANNE LABORATORIES, INC.
    P.O. Box 1738
    Columbus, Ohio 43216

176. Drug Names and Slang Terms. n.d. 11 p. Free. HS, Adults. This list was compiled from a number of sources and appeared in the "Drug Information Newsletter" of the University of Minnesota Drug Information Program.

POLICE SAFETY COUNCIL, INC.
    1602 East 73rd Street
    Indianapolis, Indiana 46240

177. This Could Happen to You in One Year. . . the Toll of Pep Drug. 1969. 5 p. Free. HS, Adults. General information and ten commandments for parents. Drug chart.

PRINCETON UNIVERSITY PRESS
    Princeton, New Jersey 08540

178. Psychedelics and the College Student. 1969.
      30 p. 50¢. Adults. A supplemented edition
with a new section on amphetamines and barbiturates.
Legal, medical, and social aspects of psychedelics,
amphetamines, and barbiturates given; the successful
and unsuccessful trip of psychedelics depicted. Counsel and information. Bibliography and glossary. Cash
must accompany all orders under a minimum of ten
copies. Special discounts apply to quantity orders;
price list available.

PROJECT DARE
     Drug Abuse Research and Education
     c/o The Neuropsychiatric Institute
     UCLA Center for the Health Sciences
     760 Westwood Plaza
     Los Angeles, California 90024

179. Distributes upon request a free and valuable pack-
et of information, including Criteria for Evaluation of
Drug Abuse Literature, Criteria for Evaluation of Drug
Education Films, magazine reprints, a question and
answer sheet on drugs, government documents, sources
of Additional Information on Narcotics and Dangerous
Drugs, a Glossary of Slang Terms Associated with
Today's Youth and Drugs of Abuse, letters from Rich-
ard Nixon and Ronald Reagan recommending Project
DARE, as well as two pamphlets entitled A Teen
D.A.R.E.: Life Can Be Exciting Without Drug Dreams
and Drugs and the Law.

PUBLIC AFFAIRS PAMPHLETS
     381 Park Avenue, South
     New York, New York 10016

*180. What About Marijuana? 1969. 21 p. illus.
       25¢. Pamphlet No. 436. By Jules Saltman.
   HS, Adults. Comprehensive information.

*181. What We Can Do About Drug Abuse. 1970. 28 p.
       illus. 25¢. Pamphlet No. 390. By Jules Saltman.
   HS, Adults. Comprehensive information.

RAMCO PUBLISHING
   287 East Sixth Street
   St. Paul, Minnesota 55101

182. The Road to Oblivion. 1969. 25 p. illus. 15¢.
   HS, Adults. Factual information on drug groups.
Also Minnesota law as pertains to each. Pamphlet
prepared with help of physicians, pharmacists, and
educators for high school students.

THE ROYAL BANK OF CANADA
   The Royal Bank of Canada Building
   Box 6001
   Montreal 1001, Quebec

183. Misuse of Drugs: Some Facts. 1968. 4 p.
   Vol. 49, No. 9. Available free in quantity "to
all those interested in receiving copies--just for the
asking."

SANTA CLARA COUNTY OFFICE OF EDUCATION
   Publications Department
   45 Santa Teresa Street
   San Jose, California 95110

*184. Drug Facts. n.d. 24 p. 25¢. HS, Adults.
   Short identification of drugs. Follows with physical and psychological effects, dependence, and with-
drawal symptoms. Gives legitimate medical uses.
Final chapter covers the impact of the law and the
student's future, and statements to ponder. Very good.

SCIENCE RESEARCH ASSOCIATES, INC.
   259 East Erie Street
   Chicago, Illinois 60611

*185. Facts About Narcotics and Other Dangerous
   Drugs. By Dr. Victor H. and Virginia E. Vogel.
No. 5-843. 1967. 56 p. illus. 88¢. HS. Tells
what drugs do to people, who starts taking them, how

addiction is treated, and what can be done to prevent
addiction.   Excellent.

SCOTT, FORESMAN & COMPANY
    1900 East Lake Avenue
    Glenview, Illinois 60025

*186. Drugs: Facts on Their Use and Abuse.   1969.
       illus.   48 p.   HS, Adults. $1. 02.   By Norman
W. Houser, director, Inner City Project, San Diego,
California, in consultation with Julius B. Richmond,
M. D.   Covers all drug divisions, the law and drug con-
trol, the problem from the standpoint of the individual,
society, medicine, etc.

SIGNAL PRESS
    School and College Service
    1730 Chicago Avenue
    Evanston, Illinois 60201

       (Signal Press publishes material: (1) useful to
educators, the clergy, other church and youth leaders,
students of social and civic problems, welfare and
safety workers, etc.   (2) Organizational and promotion-
al materials for use within the Women's Christian Tem-
perance Union.)

187. The "Dope" on Drug Abuse: A Brief Readable
      Report.   1970.   19 p.   20¢.   HS, Adults.
Adapted from "Dope on Dope" by R. V. Seliger, M. D.

188. High School Hurdles.   1968.   96 p.   illus.   75¢.
      For school administrators and other group leaders.
Heart of 6 booklets brought under one cover.   Covers
alcohol, tobacco, dope.   Written by medical and criminal authorities.

189. Some Hints for Public School Teachers: Vital
      Reasons for Teaching the Effects of Alcohol, To-
bacco, and Narcotics in the Classroom.   n. d.   4 p.
10¢.   Adults.

The 1971 catalog and "Suggested Materials for Libraries" of the Signal Press list materials for sale also that are published by Tane Press.

H. K. SIMON CO., INC.
   Box 236, Dept. BCO
   Hastings-on-Hudson, New York 10706

190. Drug Abuse: A Dead-End Street; a Student's Guide to Narcotics Information. 1969. 19 p. Samples available to educators. HS, Adults. The why, what, and who of drugs. Basic information, legal controls. By Dr. Sidney B. Birnbach, director of HPER, Yonkers (N. Y.) Public Schools. Good.

191. Let's Talk About Drugs: How They Can Help You, How They Can Harm You. 1971. 14 p. illus. Samples available to educators. Elem, HS. Questions and answers. By Dr. Sidney B. Birnbach. Good.

SMITH KLINE & FRENCH LABORATORIES [Manufacturer of Pharmaceuticals]
   Distribution Protection Section
   1500 Spring Garden Street
   Philadelphia, Pennsylvania 19101

*192. Drug Abuse: A Manual for Law Enforcement Officers. 68 p. illus. Five free copies. Provides medical use and abuse of various drug groups, discusses drugs and driving, illegal traffic, drug laws, etc. References, films, good glossary.

*193. Drug Abuse Products Reference Chart. 1968. Ten free copies. HS, Adults. Provides pharmacologic classification, law controls, medical use, potential for physical and psychological dependence, penalties, etc.

*194. Drug Abuse: The Empty Life. 1967. illus. 14 p. HS, Adults. 12 free copies.

STATE BOARD OF HEALTH

195. Usually one's State Board of Health disseminates
     materials on drug abuse.   The Indiana State
Board, for example, publishes a Chart Listing Drugs,
Medical Uses, Symptoms Produced and Their Dependent
Potentials and a sheet entitled Drug Abuse--Identifying
It. The latter covers the common symptoms of drug
abuse in students and manifestations of specific drugs.

STATE POLICE

196. Your State Police may publish a pamphlet on
     drug education.   The Indiana State Police, for
example, has for distribution a four-page pamphlet entitled Roads to Ruin--primarily a drug chart giving
basic information on drug groups.

TANE PRESS
     Texas Alcohol Narcotic Education, Inc.
     2814 Oak Lawn Avenue
     Dallas, Texas 75219

*197. Drug Abuse: Teenage Hangup; a Handbook for
      Teachers. 1971. 141 p. illus. By Donald J.
Merki, Ph.D. $1.75.   A concise and comprehensive
source to provide information to the teacher, student,
or parent about drug abuse, its history, and the pres-
ent-day dilemma.   Final chapter includes drugs and
the laws, extensive glossaries, and a bibliography.

*198. For Parents Only: A Parent's Guide on Danger-
      ous Drugs. 1971. 32 p. illus. 60¢. Adults.
Deals with each drug, causes behind drug abuse, and
positive action.   Written jointly by a psychologist, a
youth counselor, and a student working with addicts.

*199. Glue Sniffing: Big Trouble in a Tube. 1971.
      31 p. 75¢. By Lindsay R. Curtis, M.D. Car-
toon-illus. by Paul Farber. Elem., HS. Commands
attention. Informative.

*200. How About Heroin? 1971. 31 p. 75¢. By
       Lindsay R. Curtis, M.D. Cartoon-illus. by Paul
Farber. Jr. & Sr. HS. Brief history, hazards, with-
drawal symptoms, etc.

*201. LSD: Trip or Trap? 1971. 32 p. 75¢. By
       Lindsay R. Curtis, M.D. Cartoon-illus. by
Doug Dillard. HS, Adults. Endorsed by Director
Hinds, Department of Health, Education, and Welfare.
Extensive references.

*202. Let's Talk About Drugs. 1970. 16 p. illus.
       25¢. By Lindsay R. Curtis, M.D. HS, Adults.
Questions and answers concerning various drugs. Concise.

*203. Let's Talk About Goofballs and Pep Pills. 1970.
       45 p. 75¢. Written by Lindsay R. Curtis, M.D.
Cartoon-illus. by Dean Hurst. HS, Adults.

*204. Parents Guide to Marijuana. n.d. 9 p. illus.
       25¢. Adults. Members of San Jose Police De-
partment and medical doctors assisted in preparation
of this pamphlet.

*205. Why Not Marijuana? 1971. 47 p. 75¢. By
       Linday R. Curtis, M.D. Cartoon-illus. by Dean
Hurst. Jr. & Sr. HS. Well-documented research.

       The Tane Press Catalog of Educational Materials
on Problems of Dangerous Drugs, Narcotics, Alcohol,
Smoking will provide information about briefer publications, as well as a 96-page teacher's handbook entitled
The Problem: Alcohol-Narcotics and curriculum
guides. Excellent publications.

TEXTBOOK SERVICES
    2210 S.W. 3rd Street
    Miami, Florida 33132

206. Narcotics and Dangerous Drugs. 1970. 34 p.
      75¢. A student handbook for elementary school.

Ten lesson plans, each with introductory questions and
answers followed by vocabulary, unanswered questions,
activities, and sentence completion exercises.   The
conclusion covers what the student can do about drug
addiction.   Glossary of terms and a bibliography of
pamphlets for students to read.   Comprehensive and
worthy of note for self instruction by all young children.

TREND HOUSE
    P. O. Box 2350
    Tampa, Florida 33601

*207. 300 Most Abused Drugs: A Pictorial Handbook of
       Interest to Law Enforcement Officers and Others.
1970.   24 p. $2.   Arranged with pictures of tablets
and capsules laid out in color and in actual size.   By
Edward Bludworth, a registered pharmacist and drug
inspector for the Florida State Division of Health.   Excellent.

UNITED METHODIST BOARD OF CHRISTIAN SOCIAL
CONCERNS
    Service Department
    100 Maryland Avenue, N. E.
    Washington, D. C. 20002

208. Drug Abuse: Summons to Community Action
      (With 13-page supplement).   24 p.   50¢.   Adults.
Case studies of six community-school drug abuse programs, analysis of causes of drug abuse, guidelines
for organization and action, section on drugs and laws.

209. Putting the Pieces Together: A Drug Education
      Resource Book.   1970.   77 p. $1.25.   Sr. HS,
Adults.   By Thomas E. Price, Ph. D.   Informs reader
about drugs with particular focus on heroin, marihuana,
LSD, their differences and similarities and the effects
of use; drug users, who they are and why they use
various kinds of drugs; drug control laws; and therapeutic approaches.   (A four-part record, a question-
naire, and a drug chart are available with pamphlet,

making up an educational unit entitled "The Drug Puzzle Packet," $5.) Selected references, films, and filmstrips. Very good.

210. What You Need to Know About Drugs. n.d.   6-page flyer. 10¢. HS, Adults. Also available from North Conway Institute, Inc. (q.v.).

UNITED NATIONS
    New York, New York 10017

211. Estimated World Requirements of Narcotic Drugs and Estimates of World Production of Opium. 1968. 75 p. $1.50. Adults. Published by the International Narcotics Control Board and contains the estimated requirements of narcotic drugs under international control in all countries and territories of the world.

212. International Control of Drugs. 1965. 44 p. 25¢. Adults. Covers the historical background of international narcotics control and the existing system; types of narcotic drugs under international control; drug addiction and the cure and rehabilitation of addicts; suppression of illicit traffic in narcotic drugs; technical assistance in the field; and drugs outside international control.

THE UNIVERSITY OF THE STATE OF NEW YORK
    The State Education Department
    Albany, New York 12224

213. A Multimedia Reference Listing of Materials on Drug Education. 1971. 149 p. Listing includes addresses to the public, advertisements, charts, editorials, posters, audio and video tapes, audiovisual catalogs, bibliographies, books, drug education kits, essays, film reviews, films, filmstrips, general articles, pamphlets, government publications, papers, proceedings, reports, professional articles, radio and television spot announcements, serial publications, slides, sources of information on drug education, student textbooks and booklets, teach-

ers' handbooks and curriculum guides, transparencies
and overlays. Publication not available for purchase; sup-
plied on request to school districts for use in health and
drug education programs.

WASHINGTON STATE
    Office of the Governor
    Office of Program Planning and Fiscal Management
    Insurance Building
    Olympia, Washington 98501

214. Report to Governor Daniel J. Evans: The Gov-
     ernor's Task Force on Drug Abuse. 1969. 36 p.
$1. Adults. Recommendations concern education,
community responsibility, law enforcement and legal
problems, research, treatment and rehabilitation, and
coordination. Will fill requests until supply is depleted.

YALE REPORTS
    75 Howe Street
    New Haven, Connecticut 06511

215. Creativity and the Use of Drugs. 6-2-68. No.
     479. 7 p. 25¢. Adults. Rollo May, supervi-
sor of the William Alanson White Institute, speaks of
his own experience and the reports of others with LSD.

216. On Drugs. 10-19-69. No. 525. 8 p. 25¢.
     Adults. Dr. Louria, president of the New York
State Council on Drug Addiction, gives informed opinions about drug use and abuse.

YOUTH FOR CHRIST INTERNATIONAL
    Box 419
    Wheaton, Illinois 60187

217. Escape to Slavery. 1969. 17 p. 25¢. HS,
     Adults. Discusses why teens use drugs, major
drug types, drug-dependency, coping and prevention.
Religious overtones. Endorsed by Art Linkletter and
Pat Boone. Good.

GOVERNMENT DOCUMENTS

The following publications are available from the Superintendent of Documents, U. S. Government Printing Office, Washington, D. C. 20402. All items listed are limited and prices are subject to change without advance notice. Rules require remittance in advance of shipment. Check or money order should be made payable to the Superintendent of Documents. Postage stamps and foreign currency are not acceptable.

218. Amphetamines, Report by the Select Committee on Crime. (Catalog No. 91-2:H. rp.1807). 1971. 44 p. 25¢. Adults. In five parts: the speed scene--history, physical effects, psychosis, violence and crime; amphetamine abuse in Japan and Sweden; speed source and supply; controls; and recommendations.

219. Are You Just Watching. . . While Drug-Related Crime Invades Your Neighborhood? (J24.2:C86). Available free from the Bureau of Narcotics and Dangerous Drugs. 1970. 4 p. How to protect your family and neighborhood and pointers for parents.

220. Before Your Kid Tries Drugs. (FS 2.22:D 84/10). PHS Pub. 1947. NIMH. 1969. 13 p. Highly illustrated. Answers some of the most frequently-asked questions surrounding the use of marihuana, narcotics, barbiturates, and amphetamines.

221. British Drug Safety System, Report by the Committee. (91-2:H. rp 931). 1970. 100 p. 45¢.

Adults. The British and American drug systems in perspective, characteristics of the British drug safety system, origins of the British system, "Thalidomide" and British reaction, etc.

222. Community Mental Health Approach to Drug Addiction. (FS 17.2:D 84). HEW. 1968. 136 p. $1. Adults. Contents cover the American reaction to narcotics use; physical, psychological, and social aspects of addiction; the community mental health approach to diagnosis; targets, goals, and methods for intervention.

223. Community Program Guide, Drug Abuse Prevention. (J24.8:D 84/2). 20¢.

224. Directory of Narcotic Addiction Treatment Centers in the United States, 1968-1969. (HE 20. 2402:N 16/3/968-69). 1970. 162 p. $1.25. Adults. More than a detailed directory of narcotic addiction treatment agencies. Presents a comprehensive analysis of the posture of the U.S. with respect to the approaches, rationales, organization, and methods of treatment of this now endemic social disease during 1967-1969.

225. Don't Guess About Drugs, When You Have the Facts; a Description and Catalog of the Current Drug Abuse Information-Education Materials Available from the NIMH. (HE 20.2417:D 84/3). 1970. 18 p. 20¢.

226. Drug Abuse, Game Without Winners, a Basic Handbook for Commanders. (D 2.14:GEN-33). 1968. 72 p. illus. 50¢. Comprehensive information about drugs and drug abuse, recommended action and illicit channels of distribution. Index.

227. Drug Abuse Prevention: A Community Program Guide. 1970. Unpaged. 20¢. Free from Bureau of Narcotics and Dangerous Drugs. Adults. Shows how other organizations have carried out successful programs. Very good.

228. Drug Abuse--What Do You Know About It? n.d.
11 p. Available free from National Institute of
Mental Health Clinical Research Center, Lexington,
Kentucky. To nurses who are not working with drug
abuse (or who don't think they are) from nurses who
are working with it.

229. Drug-Taking in Youth: An Overview of Social,
Psychological, and Educational Aspects. (J 24. 2:
Y 8). 1971. 48 p. 40¢. Adults. Educators.
Paints a picture, based on reliable facts, of the cur-
rent phenomenon, mainly its social and psychological
aspects.

230. Drugs and You. (D2.14:FS-51). 11 p. 10¢.

231. Drugs of Abuse. (J 24. 2:D 84). 1970. 14 p.
40¢. HS, Adults. Colorful illustrations of types
of dosage and illicit forms, all of which are identified
and effects given. Drug chart covers 2-page spread.

232. Fact Sheets. (J 24.10:1-17). 1969. 45 p. 60¢.
Adults. Contains Fact Sheets 1-17 relating to
drugs and narcotics. Gives information on the Bureau
of Narcotics and Dangerous Drugs and their responsibility as to enforcement of laws and statutes relating
to drugs.

233. First Facts About Drugs. (HE 20.4015:21, FDA
Pub. 21). 1970. 9 p. 15¢. HS, Adults.

234. A Guide to Drug Abuse Education and Information
Materials. (PHS Pub. 2155). 1971. 17 p. 20¢.
Describes materials produced by National Institute of
Mental Health, as well as suggestions for communicat-
ing about drugs, using print, visual and mass media.

235. Guidelines for Drug Abuse Prevention Education.
(J 24. 8:D84/4). 1970. 77 p. 75¢. Educators.
Background information concerning considerations, phi-
losophies, approaches, and objectives of drug pro-
grams, as well as school-law enforcement cooperation.
Sample courses of study, grades 4-12.

236. Handbook of Federal Narcotic and Dangerous
     Drug Laws. (J 24. 8:N 16). 1969. 89 p. 50¢.
Adults. Designed to provide, in one place, a digest of
the Federal narcotic, marihuana, and dangerous drug
laws.

237. Heroin and the Heroin Paraphernalia, Report by
     the Select Committee on Crime. (91-2:H. rp.
1808). 1971. 83 p. 40¢. Adults. In seven parts:
history, the addiction crisis, smuggling, distribution,
heroin paraphernalia, narcotics research, and recommendations.

238. Hooked! (HE 20.2402:H 76). 1967. 31 p. 10¢.
     Graphically portrays by color cartoons the pit-
falls of a student listening to temptation and the mean-
ing of addiction. Commands interest. Spanish lan-
guage edition, Jukiado! (HE 20.2402:H 76/Spanish).

239. How Safe Are Our Drugs? (FS 13.111:44/2).
     1968. 10 p. 15¢. Educators. Curriculum re-
source guide. Suggested for use in intermediate and
secondary schools. Outlines processes of FDA's pre-
marketing approval of a new drug and the preparation
of essential labeling information. Describes those re-
sponsible for the safety of a drug product.

240. How to Plan a Drug Abuse Education Workshop
     for Teachers. (FS 2.22/15:D84). 1969. 35 p.
25¢. Ten philosophical concepts for drug abuse education, objectives of in-service training, forms of orien-
tation programs, planning and conducting the workshop,
etc.

241. How Was the Trip? (HE 20.2402:T 73, PHS Pub.
     2148). 1970. 31 p. illus. 30¢. Complete
production guide for a one-act play suitable for presentation by amateur drama groups, with suggestions
for group discussions to increase community awareness
and action. By Elizabeth Blake.

242. Is It Possible That Someone You Care About Has
     Changed for No Apparent Reason? (J 24.2:Is1).

1970.   Illustrated folder designed to use as poster.
15¢. HS.   Depicts various changes that take place in
a personality abused by drugs.

243.   Katy's Coloring Book About Drugs and Health.
       (J 24.2:K 15).   1970.   16 p.   35¢.   Kindergarten
through 4th grade.   Theme of the illustrations is "Only
Sick People Need Drugs."

244.   LSD, Some Questions and Answers.   (HE 20.2402:
       L 99/970, PHS Pub. 1828).   1970.   8-page fold-
er.   10¢.   HS, Adults.   Identifies the chemical, gives
effects, debates potentialities and possible cause of
birth defects, the law, etc.

245.   LSD-25, A Factual Account, Layman's Guide to
       Pharmacology, Physiology, Psychology and Soci-
ology of LSD.   (J 24.8:L 99/rep.).   1969.   44 p.
30¢.   Adults.

246.   Leaving the Drug World Behind.   (HE 5.225:250
       55).   Reprinted from American Education, Jan.-
Feb.   10¢.

247.   Marihuana and Health: A Report to the Congress.
       (HE 20.2402:M 3313).   1971.   176 p. $1.50.
Adults.   Covers the current status of marihuana use,
including the effects of the drug on the individual's
health.

248.   Marihuana and Health: A Report to the Congress
       from the Secretary, Department of Health, Educa-
tion and Welfare.   March, 1971.   100 p.   Cat. no.
unassigned.   Price (?).   General reader and technical-
ly sophisticated.   Summarizes what is known about
marihuana, examines its substance, the extent and patterns of use and abuse worldwide, research needs,
etc.

249.   Marihuana Fables and Facts.   (HE 20.2402:M33).
       1970.   Folder.   5¢.   HS, Adults.

250.   Marihuana, Report by the Select Committee on

Crime. (91-2:H. rp. 978). 1970. 114 p. 50¢.
Adults. Basic information, testimony by users and
authorities on the nature of marihuana, a community
survey, the problem of law enforcement, the debate on
penalties, the need for a definitive report, and a con-
clusive statement.

251. Marihuana, Some Questions and Answers. (HE
     20.2402:M33/2/970, PHS Pub. 1829). 1971. 12-
page folder. 10¢. HS, Adults. Excellent general information.

252. Mental Health Matters, Drug Abuse. (HE 20.
     2402:D 84/9, PHS Pub. 2101). 11 p. 10¢.

253. Miseria (Drug Addiction). (Spanish Version)
     (HE 20.2421:M68). 15¢.

254. The Narcotic Addict Rehabilitation Act of 1966.
     (HE 20.2402:N16/966, PHS Pub. 1782). 1969.
8-page folder. 10¢. Adults. Identifies the act, tells
who is and who is not eligible, gives provisions under
the four titles, implementation, and treatment in the
community.

255. Narcotic Drug Addiction. (FS 2.22/31:2, PHS
     Pub. 1021). 1963. 22 p. 25¢. Adults. Factual.

256. Narcotics, Some Questions and Answers. (HE
     20.2402:N16/2/970, PHS Pub. 1827). 1970. 8-
page folder. 10¢. HS, Adults. Excellent general information.

257. Public Speaking on Drug Abuse Prevention: a
     Handbook for the Law Enforcement Officer.
(J24.8:D 84/3). 1970. 49 p. illus. 30¢. Designed
to assist law officers to speak knowledgeably and effectively on the problems of drug abuse.

258. Recent Research on Narcotics, LSD, Marihuana
     and Other Dangerous Drugs. (HE 20.2402:N
16/4). 20¢.

259. Resource Book for Drug Abuse Education. (FS
     2.22:D 84/12, PHS Pub. 1964). 1969. 117 p.
$1.25. Educators. Basic information and techniques
and suggestions that experienced drug educators have
found helpful in communicating with young people.

260. Respect for Drugs. (J 24.8:D84). 1968. 157 p.
     $1.25. Adults. A community service program
sponsored by the College of Pharmaceutical Science,
Columbia University.

261. Sedatives, Some Questions and Answers. (HE
     20.2402:SE2, PHS Pub. 2098). 1970. 8-page
folder. 10¢. HS, Adults. Excellent general information.

262. Selected Bibliography for Students and Teachers
     on Drug Dependency and Drug Abuse. n.d. 6 p.
HS, Adults. Available free from National Institute of
Mental Health, Clinical Research Center, Lexington,
Kentucky. Recent books, periodicals, pamphlets, film-
strips.

263. A Selected Bibliography on Methadone. n.d. 4-
     page folder. Adults. Available free from Na-
tional Institute of Mental Health, Lexington, Kentucky.
Books and periodicals.

264. Selected Bibliography on Narcotics and the Law.
     n.d. 10 p. HS, Adults. Available free from
National Institute of Mental Health, Lexington. Pertinent statutes are listed first, with illustrative court
cases following. Then come books and pamphlets;
lastly, periodicals.

265. Slavery (to Drugs). (Black Version) (HE 20.
     2421:SL 1). 15¢.

266. Slavery (to Drugs). (White Version) (HE 20.
     2421:SL1/2). 15¢.

267. Stimulants, Some Questions and Answers. (HE
     20.2402:St5, PHS Pub. 2097). 1970. 10-page

folder. 10¢. HS, Adults. Excellent general information.

268. Strengthened Programs of International Coopera-
      tion for Halting the Illicit Supply of Drugs. (SI.
71:244, State Pub. 8531). 10¢. Adults. An address
by then Under Secretary Elliott L. Richardson. Keen
perception and eloquent expression.

269. Students and Drug Abuse. (HE 20. 2402:D 84/2).
      1969. 16 p. 25¢. Educators. Reprinted from
Today's Education, March, 1969.

270. Task Force Report: Narcotics and Drug Abuse,
      Annotations and Consultants' Papers. (Pr36. 8:L
41/N 16). 158 p. $1. Surveys problem. Stresses
need to strengthen law enforcement and gives recommendations for doing so. Appendices include articles
by various authors.

271. Teen-Age Booby Trap. 1970. Unpaged. Color
      cartoon-illustrated. Free from Bureau of Nar-
cotics and Dangerous Drugs. Elem., HS. Good overview of the history of drugs, their legitimate use and
abuse, and effects. Very readable.

272. Terms and Symptoms of Drug Abuse. (J 24. 2:D
      84/3). 35¢.

273. Things Could Be Worse, We Could Be Hung Up
      on Drugs! (D2. 9:55). 10¢.

274. The Up and Down Drugs: Amphetamines and Bar-
      biturates. (FS 2. 22:Am 7/969, PHS Pub. 1830).
1969. 8-page folder. 5¢. HS, Adults. Excellent
general information.

275. Volatile Substances: Some Questions and An-
      swers. PHS Pub. 2150. 1971. 6-page folder.
10¢. HS, Adults. Excellent general information.

276. You Think You Have Problems? (J 24. 2:P 94).
      1970. 8 p. Illustrations with comments. HS.

Compares problems of high school students with other
social ills. Shows how drugs can relieve pain and
spell tragedy as well.

277. Wanted Dead or Alive. . . Marihuana. (J 24.11:
      M 33).   20¢.

278. Wild Hemp (Marijuana), How to Control It. (A
      1. 68:969).   10¢.

279. Youth Reporters Discuss "Problem" Drugs. (HE
      21.109. 2).   1970.   46 p.   50¢.   A study of youth
opinions.

280. Youthful Drug Use. (HE 17. 2:D 84/2).   1970.
      39 p.   30¢.   Adults.   Overviews nine projects
concerning youth and drugs, etc.

REPRINTS

AMERICAN SCHOOL HEALTH ASSOCIATION
107 South Depeyster Street
Kent, Ohio 44240

The following are articles on drug abuse which
have appeared in The Journal of School Health. Reprints are 25¢ each and payment must accompany orders.

281. Drug Addiction: A Review. February, 1964,
      p. 77-87. By Albert Meyerstein, M. D.

282. Glue Sniffing, A Hazardous Hobby. May, 1964,
      p. 252. By Howard W. Pierson, M. D.

283. Psychosocial Aspects of Drug Addiction. October,
      1966, p. 481-487. By Sherwin S. Radin, M. D.

284. Junior High Seminar on Dangerous Drugs and
  •   Narcotics. February, 1968, p. 84-87. By Bar-
bara Johnson.

285. How a Health Council Developed a Narcotics Edu-
      cation Program. April, 1968, p. 243-246. By
Sanford H. Marx, Ed. D.

286. LSD: A Meaningful Approach to Drug Education.
      June, 1968, p. 386-391. By Shirley Harmon.

287. The Case Against Marijuana. October, 1968,
      p. 522-523. By Henry Brill, M. D.

288. An Evaluation of Marijuana for School Physicians, Nurses and Educators. December, 1968, p. 629-
638. By William D. Alsever, M. D.

289. Drug Use on High School and College Campuses. December, 1968, p. 638-646. By Gustav E. Cwalina, Ph. D.

290. The Teenager and Drug Abuse. December, 1968, p. 646-654. By Frank K. Johnson, M. D. and Jack C. Westman, M. D.

291. A Drug Abuse Project. December, 1968, p. 692-695. By Clifford W. Jordan.

292. Problems Related to Teaching About Drugs. February, 1969, p. 117-119. By Hester Beth Bland, H. S. D.

293. The Medico-Legal Conflict in Drug Abuse. March, 1969, p. 165-172. By Otis R. Bowen, M. D.

294. Drug Addiction--A Pharmacist's Viewpoint. March, 1969, p. 174-179. By John H. Kesling, R. Ph.

295. Innovations in Drug Education. April, 1969, p. 236-239. By Dorothy Norwalk, R. N., M. Ed.

296. Drugs in the Health Curriculum: A Needed Area. May, 1969, p. 331-337. By Mickey C. Smith, Robert L. Mikeal, and James Taylor.

297. The Central Nervous System Stimulants in Drug Abuse. June, 1969, p. 353-356. By Glenn R. Knotts, Ph. D.

298. A Clergyman Looks at Drug Abuse. September, 1969, p. 478-486. By Dr. Lycorgus M. Starkey, Jr.

299. Drugs: The Tools of Medical Progress. February, 1970. By Sue Boe, M. A.

300. Drugs on the College Campus. February, 1970, p. 91-98. By Henry B. Bryun, M.D.

301. Toward a Rational View of Drug Abuse. April, 1970, p. 192-197. By George R. Spratto, Ph.D.

302. Drug Education Begins Before Kindergarten: The Glen Cove, New York, Pilot Program. May, 1970, p. 242-248. By Mrs. Rose M. Daniels, S.N.T., M.A.

303. Patterns of Drug Use in School-Age Children. June, 1970, p. 296-301. By Harriett B. Randall, M.D.

304. A Positive Approach to Drug Education. October, 1970, p. 450-453. By Robert L. Mikeal and Mickey C. Smith, Ph.D.

305. A Graduate Student Looks at the Drug Problem. October, 1970, p. 435-437. By Ruth R. Shibuya.

306. A Scale to Measure Attitude Toward Smoking Marijuana. October, 1970, p. 454-456. By Raymond J. Vincent.

THE BILLY GRAHAM EVANGELISTIC ASSOCIATION
Box 779
Minneapolis, Minnesota 55440

307. Collecting a Blown Mind. 1970. 13 p. SC free. HS, Adults. A symposium on youth and drugs held at the headquarters of The Billy Graham Evangelistic Association, 11-12-69. Condensed from February and March, 1970, issues of Decision magazine.

BOY SCOUTS OF AMERICA
North Brunswick, New Jersey 08902

308. Drug Abuse. n.d. 4 p. 5¢. HS, Adults. By

Arthur R. Carfagni, M.D. Reprint from Scouting Magazine. Covers addicting drugs and the forms they take.

CALIFORNIA STATE DEPARTMENT OF PUBLIC HEALTH
Bureau of Health Education
2151 Berkeley Way
Berkeley, California 94704

309. Drug Abuse. April, 1970. 23 p. SC free.
Adults. A collection of updated and revised articles written and compiled by the State Department of Public Health staff in 1968, as well as some later articles taken from California's Health. Written in depth. Excellent.

THE HAIGHT-ASHBURY MEDICAL CLINIC
558 Clayton
San Francisco, California

310. Psychoactive Drugs: A Reference for the Staff of the Haight-Ashbury Medical Clinic. Vol. 1, Issue I. From Journal of Psychedelic Drugs. 16 mimeographed pages. SC free. Basically drug charts, giving as well peculiarities of administration, legitimate medical uses, potential for dependence, short and long-term effects, etc. Extensive slang glossary.

LAFAYETTE CLINIC
951 East Lafayette
Detroit, Michigan 48207

"These reprints are available free of charge to anyone." They represent all of the articles published through the Lafayette Clinic on the topic of drug abuse.

311. Auditory and Visual Threshold Effects of Marihuana in Man. Percept. Motor Skills, 29:755-759,

1969.   By D. F. Caldwell, S. A. Myers, E. F. Domino,
and P. E. Merriam.

312.   Auditory and Visual Threshold Effects of Mari-
       huana in Man: Addendum. Percept. Motor
Skills, 29:922, 1969. By D. F. Caldwell, S. A. Myers,
E. F. Domino, and P. E. Merriam.

313.   The Drug Scene in Perspective. Metro Detroit
       Sci. Review, 31:3:57-60, 1970. By S. A. Myers
and D. F. Caldwell.

314.   Effect of LSD-25 in the Rat on Operant Approach
       to a Visual or Auditory Conditioned Stimulus.
Psychol. Reports, 20:199-205, 1967. By D. F. Caldwell and E. F. Domino.

315.   Effects of Marihuana on Auditory and Visual Sen-
       sation. Michigan Mental Health Res. Bulletin.,
3:2:20-22, 1969. By S. A. Myers and D. F. Caldwell.

316.   The Effects of Marihuana on Auditory and Visual
       Sensation: A Preliminary Report. The New
Physician, 18:212-215, 1969. By S. A. Myers and D. F.
Caldwell.

317.   Effects of Marihuana Smoking on Sensory Thresh-
       olds in Man, in Psychometric Drugs. (D. H.
Efron, etc.), Raven Press, New York. By D. F. Caldwell, S. A. Myers, and E. F. Domino.

318.   The General Problem of Addiction and Habituation,
       in Drug Addiction and Habituation. (D. D. Konner,
ed.), Detroit: Wayne State University, 1968, p. 1-11.
By E. D. Luby.

319.   Heroin Addiction: A Comparison of Two Inpatient
       Treatment Methods. Michigan Med., 69:17:751-
754, 1970. By M. L. LaRouche and P. T. Donlon.

320.   Induction of Morphine Tolerance Through Inhalation
       of Morphine Alkaloid Combustion Products. Mich-
igan Mental Health Res. Bulletin., 4:1:29-31, 1970. By

S. A. Myers, F. B. Craves, and D. F. Caldwell.

321. The Marihuana Induced Social High. JAMA, 213:
8:1300-1302, 1970. By E. Rodin, E. F. Domino,
and J. Porzak.

322. A New Breed of Addict. Michigan Mental Health
Res. Bulletin., 4:4:35-36, 1970. S. A. Myers
and K. G. Schoof.

323. Psychiatrists, Marihuana and the Law: A Survey.
World J. Psychosynthesis, 2:6:1-5, 1970. By P.
Lowinger.

324. Results of Research with Marihuana: Implications
for the High School. The Human Values of Science, U. S. Army Research Office, p. 19-25, 1970.
By S. A. Myers and D. F. Caldwell.

325. Tranquilizers. Med. Trial Techn. Quart., 6:1:
19-24, 1969. By P. Lowinger.

LIFE Education Program
    Box 834, Radio City Post Office
    New York, New York 10019

    Reprints as follows are available at 35¢ each but
minimum order requirement is 15 copies.

326. Drug Abuse: Pot and Thrill Pills (# 78).

327. LSD Spells Danger (# 22).

328. Hooked on Heroin (# 87).

329. Search for Solutions (# 15).

330-333. No entries.

MEDICAL ECONOMICS, INC.
   550 Kinderkamack Road
   Oradell, New Jersey 07649

334. Drug Identification Guide. 1971. $2.50. A re-
     print from the Physician's Desk Reference.
Guide contains actual size, full-color reproductions of
the most commonly prescribed drug products, as well
as some available without prescription.

NARCOTICS EDUCATION, INC.
   P.O. Box 4390
   6830 Laurel Street, NW
   Washington, D.C. 20012

     LISTEN Magazine Reprints

335. Drugs and Driving. Vol. 23, No. 3. 4 p. 10¢.
     HS, Adults. Chart showing how drugs may be
obtained, what they are prescribed for, direct, possible, and contributory side effects, effect when com-
bined with alcohol, driving recommendations. Tips on
driving by Stirling Moss.

336. Instant Insanity: What We Know About LSD. Vol.
     21, No. 2 and Vol. 23, No. 6. 23 p. 10¢.
HS, Adult. Very good.

337. LSD: A Trip Without a Return Ticket? Vol. 20,
     No. 9. 4 p. 5¢. By Colleen Curtis.

338. Marijuana: To Go to Pot, or Not? Vol. 22, No.
     2. 23 p. 10¢. HS, Adults. Views of three
medical doctors and a user, brief excerpts from ex-
perts, and six points of the LaGuardia Report of 1944.

339. Modern Trojan Horse. Vol. 23, No. 10. 8 p.
     10¢. Adults. By Lindsay R. Curtis, M.D. In-
formation about abused drugs and why they become dangerous.

340. Pills: What Do They Mean to You? Vol. 23,

No. 10. 10¢. HS, Adults. Capsules and pills
laid out in actual size and color, giving pertinent
information about stimulants and depressants and dangers of overdosage.

341. What Drugs Are and What They Do. Vol. 20,
No. 11. 8 p. 10¢. Adults. Brief glimpse at
major popular drugs and their effects on the human
system.

Narcotics Education, Inc. publishes a catalog,
listing films, books, periodicals, and pamphlets on alcohol, drugs, and smoking. Besides Listen magazine
reprints, Tane pamphlets are also available. See Tane
Press.

THE NATIONAL RESEARCH BUREAU, INC.
424 N. Third Street
Burlington, Iowa 52601

342. First Facts About Drugs. n.d. 15 p. 25¢.
HS, Adults. Reprint from FDA Publication 21.

343. Marijuana: Is It Worth the Risk? 1969. 15 p.
illus. 25¢. HS, Adults. Reprinted from Family
Health, October Issue.

344. The Menace of Drug Abuse. n.d. 11 p. 25¢.
HS, Adults. Reprint from Pacific Telephone
Magazine.

345. What Teenagers Should Know About Narcotics.
n.d. 11 p. 25¢. HS, Adults. Reprinted from
Listen. Written by Edward R. Bloomquist, M.D.

NATIONAL SAFETY COUNCIL
425 North Michigan Avenue
Chicago, Illinois 60611

346. Drugs and the Driver. n.d. 4 p. SC free.
Available in quantity lots. HS, Adults. Reprint

from Traffic Safety Magazine.   Written by Dr. C. J.
Rehling, toxicologist for the State of Alabama.

THE READER'S DIGEST
    Pleasantville, New York 10570

    A drug reprint series, 14 in number, is available
from Reader's Digest for the price of $1.   Multiple
copies of any one article are available at prices listed
on the back of each reprint.   The series follows:

347. Afterflash.   December, 1969.   6 p.

348. An Anti-Drug Program That Works.   March,
      1971.   4 p.

349. "But, Mom, Everybody Smokes Pot!"   December,
      1968.   6 p.

350. Cool Talk About Hot Drugs.   November, 1967.
      8 p.

351. Doctor, What About Marijuana?   April, 1971.
      6 p.

352. The Drug "Trip"--Voyage to Nowhere.   August,
      1969.   4 p.

353. How California Is Licking Drug Addiction.   Sep-
      tember, 1967.   6 p.

354. How to Talk With Your Teen-Ager About Drugs.
      August, 1970.   4 p.

355. Let's Halt Heroin at the Source.   May, 1971.
      6 p.

356. Pills, Glue and Kids: An American Tragedy.
      June, 1966.   6 p.

357. The Tempting Siren Called "Speed."   October,
      1970.   6 p.

358. The Truth About LSD. September, 1966. 4 p.

359. We Must Fight the Epidemic of Drug Abuse!
     February, 1970. 6 p.

360. Where Addicts Become Adults. December, 1970.
     6 p.

THE STUDENT ASSOCIATION FOR THE STUDY OF
HALLUCINOGENS, INC.
    638 Pleasant Street
    Beloit, Wisconsin 53511

361. Drugs of Abuse: An Introduction to Their Ac-
     tions and Potential Hazards. 1970. 13 p. 50¢.
Adults. Written by Dr. Samuel Irwin, professor of
psychopharmacology at the University of Oregon Medical School. Reprint from the J. of Psychedelic Drugs.

TALBERT HOUSE [A Guidance Residence for Released
Offenders]
    2316 Auburncrest
    Cincinnati, Ohio 45219

362. Behavior in Ex-Addict Female Prisoners Participat-
     ing in a Research Study. May, 1969. 9 p. Free.
Adults. Reprint from Comprehensive Psychiatry. By
Sheldon S. Stoffer, Joseph D. Sapira, and Betty F.
Meketon.

363. Marihuana Smoking in the United States. Septem-
     ber, 1968. 8 p. Free. Adults. Reprint from
Federal Probation. By Donald D. Pet and John C. Ball.

364. Methadone Maintenance Treatment Program: A
     Description and Evaluation of a Hospital-Based
Program for the Treatment of Heroin Addicts. 1969.
6 p. Free. Adults. Reprint from Hospitals. By
Paul R. Torrens.

365. New Directions in Treating Narcotic Addicts.

February, 1970.   5 p.   Free.   Adults.   Reprint
from the Mental Health Digest.   By Harold T. Conrad.

Talbert House also sent other publications which
are available directly elsewhere.

THE YALE LAW JOURNAL CO.
401A Yale Station
New Haven, Connecticut 06520

366.   Methadone Maintenance for Heroin Addicts.   1969.
36 p. $1.   Adults.   Reprint from The Yale Law
Journal.   Discusses the medical controversy of methadone and problems under federal law.   By Paul D.
Gewirtz.

LATE ADDITIONS

AMERICAN OSTEOPATHIC ASSOCIATION
  Editorial Department
  212 East Ohio Street
  Chicago, Illinois 60611

*367. Drugs: Use and Misuse. March, 1971, issue of
  Health magazine. 63 p. illus. 10¢. HS,
Adults. A collection of articles by various authors de-
voted entirely to the drug scene. Background material, specific drugs and their effects, drug misuse as a
part of the social situation, a testimonial by a young
girl on pep pills, Congress and the passing of new
drug legislation, some viewpoints on the complex problem of drug abuse, the acute drug reaction and its
treatment, trends in drug use, human involvement as
an antidote to drugs, and suggestions for educators.
Excellent.

BETHANY FELLOWSHIP, INC.
  6820 Auto Club Road
  Minneapolis, Minnesota 55431

368. What Every Teenager Should Know About Drugs.
  1968. 55 p. 39¢. By David Wilkerson. Case
histories of drug abuse, the controversy over legalization of marijuana, general information about various
drugs.

THE BROTHERS EDUCATIONAL PUBLICATIONS CO.,
INC.
    1133 Broadway - Suite 416
    New York, New York 10010

*369. The Now Drug Scene: What Every Teenager and
       Parent Should Know. 1970. 24 p. $1 plus
postage. Beautiful color illustrations of drug and dosage forms, addict's equipment, actual-size capsules
and tablets. Information covers "Some Effects of a
Conviction for a Narcotic Felony," the problem, the
abusers, and the Federal Law. There are guidelines
for community action and advice for parents. Physical
and psychological effects for various drug groups and
social and therapeutic implications of methadone maintenance are given. Drug chart covers two-page spread.
Glossary of terms from the drug scene. This pamphlet
has received letters of endorsement from the following
institutions: Pinkerton's, Inc., Police Department of
the City of New York, New Jersey State Department of
Education, International Business Machines, and the
United States Department of Justice.

COMMUNITY SERVICE SOCIETY OF NEW YORK
    Department of Public Affairs
    105 East 22 Street
    New York, New York 10010

370. A Study of Four Voluntary Treatment and Reha-
      bilitation Programs for New York City's Narcotic
Addicts: The Long Road Back from a Living Death.
1967. 52 p. $1. Adults. The five chapters cover
Current Approaches to Drug Addiction, Treatment in a
Drug-Infested Environment, The Potential in an Isolated
Communal Setting, Rehabilitation Through Religious
Conversion, and The Community as Part of the Reha-
bilitation Process.

COUNCIL OF PLANNING LIBRARIANS
    Box 229
    Monticello, Illinois 61856

371. **Forces Against Drug Abuse:** Education, Legislation, Rehabilitation: A Selected Bibliography.
1971. 11 p. $1.50. Adults. By Nan C. Burg, Librarian. This bibliography grew out of the research done by the Pennsylvania Department of Community Affairs "to present to the local government official a coordinated picture of the drug problem and to suggest to him what help is available for his community and where he can receive this help." Includes pamphlets, magazine and newspaper articles, books, proceedings, government publications, etc.

KEMPER INSURANCE GROUP
    Public Relations Department
    4750 Sheridan Road
    Chicago, Illinois 60640

372. **What About Drugs and Employees?** n.d. 13 p.
    5 copies free; additional copies 10¢ each. Adults.
By Lewis F. Presnall. This booklet delineates formal policy of the Kemper organization regarding on-the-job instances of drug traffic and drug abuse.

LEASCO RESPONSE INCORPORATED
    5401 Westbard Avenue
    Washington, D.C. 20016

373. **Controlling Drug Abuse Programs.** 1971. 12 p.
    SC free. Adults. By Jerry L. Holden. Discusses the basic elements of a proposed electronic data processing network installed at local treatment centers. The local urban system, identified as metronet would intercommunicate among neighboring treatment centers and build into state or regional networks. Suggested as the solution to record-keeping problems at community-based drug treatment clinics. . . an effort to maximize the time and effectiveness of the physician, nurse, psychiatrist, counselor, etc.

LOS ANGELES COUNTY
    Department of Community Services
    Narcotic Information Service
    220 North Broadway
    Room 701
    Los Angeles, California 90012

374. Darkness on Your Doorstep: A Report to Parents
     on Juvenile Drug Abuse. 1969. 25 p. illus.
Free. Informs parents why children turn to drugs, of
their availability, the legal consequences, and danger
signals to be alerted to in recognizing abuse. Drug
groups are covered with accompanying color illustrations of tablets and capsules laid out in actual size.
Last section tells parents how they can help.

MEDIA FAIR/U.S. EDUCATIONAL MARKETING COR-
PORATION
    29 Poplar Drive
    Stirling, New Jersey 07980

375. Publishes price list and catalog, offering AP
     Booklet: What You Should Know About Drugs and
Narcotics, $1, listed under Associated Press, and
many other items, such as flip charts with accompanying instructor's manual, photographs with teacher's
guide, flannel board, oversize pills, tablets, capsules,
facsimile of the marijuana plant, etc.

MOTIVATION, INC.
    P.O. Box 4695
    Stamford, Connecticut 06907

376. A Trip to Nowhere. 1970. 32 p. 50¢. (Quan-
     tity lot prices given on request). HS, Adults.
By James E. Crane, M.D. Overview of drug problem,
addiction defined and general symptoms of abuse given.
Physical consequences and why people turn to drugs
outlined. Specific drugs described and effects of abuse
stated.

NASSAU (COUNTY OF)
    Police Department
    Mineola, New York 11501

377. Drug Abuse. n.d. 16 p. SC free. HS, Adults.
    Describes the pitfalls and effects of drug abuse,
Nassau County's problem, the drugs themselves. Gives
symptoms, legal aspects, and tells where to go for
help in that area.

NATIONAL COUNCIL OF CHURCHES
    Department of Ministry
    475 Riverside Drive
    New York, New York 10027

378. Pastoral Care of Young Drug Users and Their
    Families. 1971. 30 p. SC free; additional
copies 10¢ each. Adults. By John D. Spangler. Factual knowledge outlined that the pastor needs to know
about youth and their problems as related to drug abuse,
as well as suggestions as to how he can help the individual abuser by working with him and his family, as-
sessing the situation and setting realistic goals. Bibliography. Very good.

NATIONAL SCHOOL PUBLIC RELATIONS ASSOCIATION
    1201 16th Street, N.W.
    Washington, D.C. 20036

379. Should Teens Smoke? Drink? Take Drugs?
    1969. 11 p. 25¢. Quantity lot prices available.
Payment must accompany orders for $2 or less. By
Rose Marie Walker. Deals mainly with the proper way
to educate and influence youth concerning the use of
tobacco, liquor, and drugs.

PENNSYLVANIA (COMMONWEALTH OF)
    Department of Health
    Division of Drug Control
    P.O. Box 90
    Harrisburg, Pa. 17120

380. <u>Desk Reference on Drug Abuse for Teachers.</u>
     n.d.   17 p.   SC sent free; no price given.   Def-
initions of types of drug dependency; characteristics of
drug dependence as relates to the different types; ra-
tionale, basic concepts, suggested pupil outcomes, and
selected references and resources for an instructional
program; common symptoms of drug abuse and manifestations of specific drugs; glossary of drug slang.

381. <u>Drug Dependency.</u>   1971.   7 mimeographed sheets.
     SC sent free; no price given.   Defines drug de-
pendence generally and psychic and physical dependency
specifically.   Characteristics of different types of drug
dependence, such as the morphine type, alcohol type,
etc.   Information condensed from several sources.

382. <u>Forces Against Drug Abuse: Education, Legisla-
     tion, Rehabilitation: A Selected Bibliography.</u>
Revised, November 1971.   11 p.   SC sent free; no
price given.   By Nan C. Burg, Librarian of the Department of Community Affairs Library.   Also available
from Council of Planning Librarians.

383. <u>A Local Officials' Guide to Combating Drug Abuse.</u>
     1971.   SC sent free; no price given.   57 p.
"The purpose of this manual is to provide local government officials and community leaders with basic information about the drug abuse problem and to suggest
ways to proceed to combat it in their communities.
The manual is not intended to be detailed or technical
in nature.   Rather it is a basic publication to guide
community leaders to the technical sources and ex-
pertise available to them."

384. <u>Marijuana.</u>   n.d.   9 p.   SC sent free; no price
     given.   HS, Adults.   Defines marijuana and hash-
ish.   Tells how marijuana is prepared, how it works,
what the physical and mental reactions are, its dependency, the laws governing it, and a brief note about its
legalization.

385. <u>Narcotics.</u>   n.d.   8 p.   SC sent free; no price
     given.   HS, Adults.   General information about

opium and its active components: morphine, heroin, codeine, as well as cocaine and marijuana which for legal purposes are classified as narcotics. Brief information also on the synthetic drugs of Meperidine and Methadone. Two-page chart giving "Slang Terms," "How Taken," and "How to Spot an Abuser" on Commonly Abused Narcotics.

386. What a Young Person Can Do to Help Stop the Spread of Drug Abuse. n.d. Broadside. SC sent free; no price given. Eleven ways outlined to help stop the spread of drug abuse.

QUEENS COUNTY
    Office of the District Attorney
    125-01 Queens Boulevard
    Kew Gardens, Jamaica, New York 11415

387. My kid? Never! n.d. 2 p. Distributed to all community organizations at no charge. May be reprinted as long as proper acknowledgments are made. An Eye-on-Crime Narcotics Identification Chart covering drug used, physical symptoms, what to look for, and dangers.

SEABURY BOOKSTORE
    815 Second Avenue
    New York, New York 10017

388. On Pills and Needles: A Christian Look at Drug Dependence. 1969. 36 p. Examination copy free. Additional copies 50¢ each; $40 per hundred. Adults. By Kenneth W. Mann, specialist in the field of religion and psychology. Includes such aspects as the use and control of drugs. A note to the reader presents an interesting theory as to the healthy and unhealthy dependencies and how the latter leads to drug abuse. "This handbook is about the risky substances people become dependent upon, what their effects and withdrawal symptoms are, what issues of personality development toward freedom are involved, and what we in the church can do about it."

H. K. SIMON CO., INC.
    Box 236
    Hastings-on-Hudson, New York 10706

389. <u>Drinking, Drugs and Driving.</u> 1971 SC free.
       <u>Available in quantity lots.</u> Price list available.
HS, Adults. By Charles R. Self in consultation with
Frank A. Seixas. Explains why young drivers are
greater traffic accident risks; discusses drinking and
driving, drugs and drink, mental clarity and driving,
why we drink or take drugs, various drugs and their
effects. Logically written to appeal to youth.

TENNESSEE (STATE OF)
    Legislative Council Committee
    State Capitol
    Nashville, Tennessee 37219

390. <u>Study on Narcotics and Drug Abuse.</u> 1970. 176 p.
       SC sent free; no price given. Adults. An in-
depth study by the Legislative Council Committee of the
"nature and degree" of the drug problem in the state of
Tennessee. Includes also source information, conclu-
sions, and recommendations.

TEXAS STATE PROGRAM ON DRUG ABUSE
    Mr. Walter Richter, Director
    Executive Department
    Littlefield Building
    Austin, Texas 78711

391. <u>Guidelines for Community Action on Drug Abuse.</u>
       n. d. 32 p. SC free. "This booklet is designed
as a guideline for initiation of community action in at-
tacking the problem and as a handbook for information
resources and sources for aid. It will provide specific
information for communities in Texas."

TIME EDUCATION PROGRAM
    Time & Life Building

Rockefeller Center
New York, New York 10020

*392. A Time Guide to Drugs and the Young. 1970.
23 p. $1.50. For every parent ... for every
teacher. By Christopher Cory, Ray Godfrey, and Jane
Stavsky. Contents cover patterns of and reasons for
drug abuse, drugs and their dangers, drug laws, toward a drugless turn-on (guidelines for discussion, prevention and early treatment), suggestions for the classroom and a bibliography of books, pamphlets, films,
and magazine articles. Stresses that the answer to the
problem is education--an honest appraisal of the drugs
themselves and of the values by which we live. Appeals
to the community not to close its eyes and pretend that
no problem exists. Two master ditto sheets give two
views of 17-year olds who turned on.

UNIVERSITY OF THE PACIFIC
School of Pharmacy
Stockton, California 95204

393. Drug Abuse Education: Teachers and Counselors.
1970. SC sent free; no price given. 155 p. A
compilation of the presentation made at the Drug Abuse
Institute for Teachers and Counselors June 7-12, 1970,
University of the Pacific, School of Pharmacy. Contents cover Introduction and Keynote Address, The Drug
Problem and Its Dimensions; Drug Information; Legal
and Moral Aspects of Drug Abuse; and Approaches to
the Drug Problem.

WADSWORTH PUBLISHING COMPANY, INC.
10 Davis Drive
Belmont, California 94002

394. The Use and Misuse of Drugs: A Social Dilemma. 1970. 86 p. Text price 95¢. Trade price
$1.25. Basic Concepts in Health Science Series.
Eight chapters cover: 1) Introduction; 2) Drugs: Problems, Considerations, and Definitions; 3) Drug Users:

Their Characteristics, Patterns of Drug Use, and Behavior; 4) Drugs: Types, Uses, and Effects; 5) Misuse of Drugs and the Community's Response; 6) Treatment and Legal Control of Drug Use; 7) Economics of
Drug Use and Misuse; 8) Further considerations, Annotated Bibliography, Glossary, and Index.

AUTHOR INDEX

TITLE INDEX

SUBJECT INDEX

Bibliography

Charts and Glossaries

Church's Mission

Community Programs and Guides

Depressants

Drugs and Driving

General

Guides for Parents

Hallucinogens

Information Handbooks and Teaching Guides

Institutes

Laws and Law Enforcement

Narcotic Habit--General

Narcotic Habit--Treatment and Rehabilitation

Pictorial Works

Research

Special Publications

Stimulants